I0098284

Prescription To Destiny

Terri D. McLennan
Triple Seven Press • Las Vegas, NV • 2003

ISBN 0-9710486-3-0

Published by Triple Seven Press, PO Box 70552, Las Vegas, NV 89170. http://www.777press.com

Special thanks to Laurie L. Shaw for assistance with cover design.

To contact the author, please e-mail tdm619@yahoo.com.

WARNING AND DISCLAIMER

Prescription To Destiny can be special-ordered through Ingram and is available online at Amazon.com.

Dedication

This book is dedicated to the Higher Power of my life and to my sons who have consoled me throughout their existence in my life.

I thank God for granting them to me, as I asked for them specifically. It is my desire to see them do well in this life. I know that they can if they listen to the Spirit, the Helper that is given to us all.

There is a Higher Power in all our lives. It is the entity that gives us life and allows everything living around us to exist.

Contents

Foreword

Prescription To Destiny is the first book by a very talented and articulate writer, poet, and spiritual teacher, Ms. Terri D. McLennan. I have known Terri for a number of years and our conversations about the spiritual promptings for the creation of this work are still fond memories fresh in my mind. I am honored to have the privilege of writing the foreword to the primal stirrings of this brilliant creative spirit. Terri is certainly to become a force to be reckoned with in the writing world.

What is destiny? What is Spirit? In today's world, the examination of such lofty philosophical questions and concepts almost seems parenthetical. We tend to become engrossed in the material to such an extent that matters of Spirit become relegated to the corners of an often-ignored daydream. In the repetition of this existentialist malaise, we all too often give up the most beautiful and potentially fulfilling part of who we are, the Spirit. In this work, Terri tackles the question head on. What would life be like if we placed our innermost spiritual urges at the forefront of our consciousness? Could we discover the meanings within life that we so desperately seek to uncover? Through our mental servitude to the various and sundry manipulations that the world would have us believe, we stop looking for truth. It becomes something that we simply do not have time for.

Terri often challenges her readers to examine some small detail of life that we would normally overlook. Sometimes this level of detailed examination is painful, and to some extent, even traumatic. But when you travel with her on this journey, you discover something wonderful about the need for such depth of introspection; it is the language that your very spirit uses to define your life. All too often, we give up the details of life to the fate of the universe. How many times have you heard a friend say, "Everything will be all right somehow"? Such thinking, according to Terri, negates the power and majesty of a well-orchestrated discourse between the Spirit and the conscious mind. In the process of detailed self-examination, we discover the power of Spirit busily working away at designing exactly that life that we yearn for.

As you read *Prescription To Destiny*, one gets the sense that you are talking with a soul that has taken the time to sit with her indwelling spirit and demand that it teach her its secrets. Such secrets are not easily rendered as the life of the author portends from her intense emotional struggles as a girl to the battles that she engages within her troubled relationships as an adult. Through it all, one gets the sense of a great spirit teaching, molding, and guiding the struggling human being toward a more meaningful and compassionate future. The Prescription we find is to listen, to pray, and to care.

Mitchell E. Gibson, M.D.
Phoenix, Arizona
Author of *Medicine for the Soul* and *Remembering Inner Peace*

Acknowledgments

I'd like to give special thanks to all those who helped me throughout my life:

My foster parents Frank & Madie Montgomery for loving me when I needed it.

A very special Lady and educator in the McLennan County School District, and the last foster parent I would encounter, Aria Marie Thompson, who loves, is compassionate, gentle, and one of the loveliest spirits I know. You have been a wonderful blessing to me. I will NEVER forget the love you extended to me. You told me one thing that I will never forget. "You can be whatever you want to be." Thank you for loving me.

All my teachers as well as those who told me "No, you CAN'T do it!" You inspired me and at age 12, I learned that "Yes, I can."

My big sister Mentha. You may not know this but honey, I have always listened to you. When you told me things, I listened and followed through. Thank you for all those days of support.

All my other siblings for setting examples that I learned from and all my friends and relatives for acknowledging the uniqueness I gave to the family.

I don't want to forget you, Wendy Y. Tucker, for believing in me, as well as having the patience to work with me to complete this project.

I'd like to thank Dr. Mitchell Gibson, M.D., for his friendship and counsel while I was learning to put my energies together for this book. His opinions and leadership gave me the inspiration not only to do my best, but also the fortitude to believe in the Higher Powers of inner self and spirituality that guide and prompt us to listen and to care.

Last but not least, I want to thank my mother and father Cecil and Effie Mae, for my birthright. When they were told I would not live, they said otherwise, "Yes, she will."

Thank you all so very much. When I cease to exist in this mortal life I will continue to live through this message and the encouragements I leave with you. I hope that knowing me has made a difference in all the lives I have touched.

I love you all.

Introduction

When you think about your future, do you think in terms of your destiny? Do you believe your life is predetermined or do you try to direct your own destiny? Do you plan for your life everyday? Do you do life or is life doing you? Are you spontaneous or do you plan everything down to the minute? How open-minded are you? Are you free? How do you know?

Many people wake each day and do not have a clue about what is going on around them. I was especially alarmed when I actually started watching people and their actions. I discovered a very insecure human nature afflicting some people. Not just some people, but many people. As I continued to educate myself, I have tapped into the cerebral processes and pondered why I waste so much valuable time. I recalled all the questions I asked my self as a child, especially, "What will I look and be like when I'm 40?" as I looked at my parents when they told me they were 40. Now that I am 40, I look at myself and wonder what I looked like when I was 10.

I failed to take a picture of myself and store it in my mind for future reference. Wouldn't it be something if we could actually do that? That is, capture our images mentally. Yet, if we could, would we remember to bring forth the images from our memory?

I believe we can if we want to. We can do everything we want to do all the time. We can use more of our minds if given the capacity to do so. We can enjoy more of our life instead of just settling for survival.

Do you know why you are alive? Again, do you know why you are alive? I encourage you to look deep down into your self, your inner man, your being , your spirit, then ask, "Do I know this part of myself? Do I know my spirit? Do I really know my spirit? Do I speak to it daily and do I listen to it when it speaks to me?"

As we proceed, I will introduce methods for communicating with your spirit and helping it to grow. If you desire to say yes to any of the questions above and to grow in nature and spirit, you can create a prescription to your destiny.

❧ 1 ☙
The Application

B.F. Skinner, Piaget, Erickson and other psychoanalytic theorists have asserted that we develop our personalities by age five or six. Therefore, most people reading this book will have already passed the personality development stage. Oh well! I hope we all had functional, intelligent, and informed parents. "Yeah right!"

However, if you had hard-working parents like I had—hard-working, common-society parents, who whipped ou asses when we were misbehaving; gave us morals, boundaries, and restrictions; and just a hope for opportunity and success in the future—then you're blessed that their trial and error worked and blessed to have gotten this far in life. There are some who don't make it.

After reading this book, you will be able to employ some of these methods in your own life and in your child's life to help him or her to grow wiser, not just older. At some point in our lives, we undoubtedly say, "I wish I knew then what I know now." Is that impossible? I think not.

There were probably warning signs, flags, and other emotions going on at the time of your alleged lack of knowledge. Whether you recognized those emotions, which I like to call sensory perceptions, is the question.

Is your inner radar so weak from lack of attention that you cannot hear it or feel it? Are you leaning on your own understanding? Does that understanding give you peace?

In applying the methods of increasing your ability to be more sensitive to the auras that give us warning and judgment abilities, it is necessary to be free, open, and truthful. Being true to yourself is very important in maintaining a relationship with your inner man, your being, and your spirit. You know when you're not honest and your spirit does too. It suffers when you are not true.

After a long period of neglect, it adjusts to a silent down mode. It does not matter how your inner self jars your mind causing you to wring your hands, pick your nose, scratch, or move excessively when you're not being truthful. You ignore these signs and continue with your neglectful attitude and character. It does not mean you are a bad person, but rather an untruthful one. It only means that you're not in touch with yourself and if you continue in this manner, you may lose yourself to reprobation.

In order to become the most of who you can be, you must be true to yourself in all things. Being true to yourself gives life abundantly with freedom and peace. Imagine getting all that simply by doing yourself some justice, by only speaking the truth. If you do not know something, then don't say you do. Only good, honest, edifying words should come out of your mouth. Words of humor and well wishes should be on your tongue.

What is the purpose of deceptive propaganda? Are we as a people really interested in a lie? No, I think not! I believe that we as a people are hungry for the truth. We want to know what our fate is. If you had a chance to do anything in the world with a guaranteed promise for success, would you want that promise built on an untruthful foundation?

The very life you have, you have it now. What you do as you go forward to the next minute, hour, or day is what will make the difference between you and your spirit, your family, and everyone else with whom you come in contact. Can you trust yourself? When you say you're going to do something, do you keep your promise to yourself? Do you put things off—important things like improving your health habits? We can always do better if we only just acknowledge ourselves—our inner man, our being, and our spirit. One of the most important steps in improving your way of life is acknowledging yourself. Being true to yourself and to others is the first step in the application of life. You may wonder, "What is meant by true?" *True* is living with everything around you in light and full awareness—your family, your surroundings, and the world.

Can you look around you at this very moment and remove things that are not pleasing to you? Do you put up with things to keep peace? If you do, you are not true to yourself. Again, being true to yourself means having all the things around you that please you. That does not mean that you can dismiss your family, your job, or your life if you are upset one day about an issue. Love your family, participate in your life, be responsible for your happiness, and be long-suffering and patient.

As a leader in your world, you are the one who will make your world proper; i.e., proper for you. As you apply the Application to your life, you will generate more happiness with yourself. More freedom, more peace. Never put the responsibility of your happiness on someone else—you'll end up unhappy nine times out of 10. If someone tells you he or she can make you happy, ask if he or she can do a better job than you can. Only then will you see where they stand.

The Application is a series of events that one must do to achieve a sense of self and well being. Applying the Application is the beginning. By applying the Application, you open doors for whatever you let in. I suggest having a long talk with the Author of your life—whoever you think is the mastermind of your creation. Empty your self out and forgive your self for self-negligence. Ask the Spirit to awaken within you, open your eyes, and allow you to see the life in the trees, the grass, the flowers, and all those things around you that live.

Make a promise to yourself and promise to fulfill that promise. Plan how you're going to find love within yourself and how you're going to give the love that overflows within to someone else. Make plans to wake up each day laughing—that is the most wonderful thing. Tell yourself from now on that all you want to see in others is good. I believe people act in aggressive or ignorant ways due to past hurts and let-downs. They've let themselves down by waiting on someone else to come through for them so they can get started on a goal. Getting started comes from you and you alone. The Spirit can call all day but you must acknowledge it to get started.

People that have been hurt usually act in a way that hurts others or perpetuates the hurt in their life. This hurt is manifested by making bad choices. If we choose to love ourselves, then we should treat ourselves as though we love ourselves. We love ourselves by making smart informed choices and getting our answers from within, not as a result of outside persuasion or convincing. If you feel confusion or doubt when making a decision, reconsider your options based on how you feel, not on how others feel, before making a commitment. What gives the persuader the right to know you better than you know yourself?

If a person can empty his mind of issues and situations that cannot be changed, he can make room for a level of freedom very few achieve. When you realize your purpose in life, and the real freedom that acknowledgment, truth, and goodwill give, you will have power over your own life. (Remember you're practicing goodwill, truth, acknowledgment, forgiveness, and love.) You will be ready to face the day. Emptying out means to forgive yourself as of right now—you have a clean slate. From the moment you read this and go your way, you start with a free and clean state of being. Acknowledgment does this. Forgive and be forgiven. Your transgressions are paid for today, tomorrow, next week—no matter what—as long as you acknowledge the spirit that lives inside of you and listen to, feel, and recognize the love. Tell yourself, "I am forgiven. I have the same opportunity in life as the pope and the next person." Everyday that we wake to a sane mind, we have an opportunity to live a more powerful life. A life of freedom, love, forgiveness, happiness, control, acknowledgment, and truth. This is the Application.

Apply those rules to your life. Remember you are free and clean. Are you smiling yet? Do you feel anything? You will when you discover that the person you thought you despised suddenly looks just like you, with the same odds in life you have. It's not based on wealth or material matter. It's a spiritual thing.

Using the Application can be difficult in certain circumstances. However, if you practice truth and deal with the associated consequences when applying the conditions of the Application, your freedom will be preserved and you won't have to shoulder that particular issue. Self-preservation is the first law of nature. Self-preservation will not allow you to harm yourself. Self-preservation is the promise to yourself that you will treat yourself like you love yourself.

> *I will only practice in truth,*
> *regardless of what your position is.*
> *I will be true to mine.*
> *— Terri D. McLennan*

Acknowledgment + Forgiveness + Truth + Love + Goodwill = Peace

Imagine if everyone in your world acted this way toward each other. Consider that world. Which world would you rather live in? The current one we live in or one evolved by acknowledgment, forgiveness, truth, love, good will, and peace.

If you don't care about yourself, maybe you shouldn't be reading this book. Perhaps you should instead seek psychological help to come to terms with why you don't. Meanwhile, if you proceed, you have a clean slate, a renewed opportunity to employ this application in your life, and a chance to give this same application to the closest person to you. This application can be practiced everyday with everyone for the rest of your life, if you desire to grow.

If you feel ill feelings from past experiences, dismiss them—tell them they are gone. Today is a whole new day, new situation, and new person, so with acknowledgment, these ill feelings will flee from you. Acknowledgment requires you to employ it to see its value. Then you will use it repeatedly with success each time.

It's amazing that I never knew how much was in me until I gave away the fight for my life. Suddenly, I realized that it wasn't my fight to begin with. I had taken on the burden of my human nature before I was introduced to my spiritual nature. I wasted time with stupid mistakes, denying myself. Then when I turned around to look at myself, I found myself lacking desire. Undoubtedly, I put myself in that position through neglect of my own needs. We need to be strong, true, and good to ourselves and we must protect ourselves. Staying out of our own way is a good thing. You do not have to be a part of the show to see it.

When you employ the Application in your life, you will be surprised at how much time you will begin to have on your hands. It's amazing how this happens. When you hear the term born again, if you don't already, you will relate. You have acknowledged who you are and who lives inside of you. You now have a relationship with your spirit, your helper, and your friend. After sometime of practicing, you will find that there will be less "shoulda, woulda, couldas" and more "I did the right thing. My mind is clear. I did what was best for me."

We all must take responsibility for ourselves and ou well-being by not exposing ourselves to conditions unde which we can't function for as long as is required. Doing so prevents lies or excuses, as we sometimes call them. There is no trick to gaining peace and happiness. All you have to do is practice truth. Are the things you do everyday truthful and within the guidelines of the society you live in, or should I say legal? If not, maybe it's time to find that place of truth. Honesty is a good thing too. It will help in the peace department and foster happiness as well

Each entity of the Application intertwines and forms a wheel, each being a spoke of support. All entities must function well in order for the whole application to work in your life. Trying to apply one without the others is sometimes referred to as splitting the post, hypocritical, two-faced, fork-tongued, fake. You get the message? We must remain real with ourselves. In order for our spirit to flourish in its freedom, it truly has to be free of the issues that give rise to guilt, condemnation, and dishonesty. It's not a fact of being right, but being true as you know it.

Discovery is a good thing. You may discover that your intuitions were wrong or right. When you know the difference and act accordingly, you seal your knowledge and faith. If you know how to do a task correctly, wouldn't you do it that way? Or would you continue to operate in a dysfunctional manner? Most people would not. If I have been going to work using a particular route for months and I find a shorter, better route, would I take it? Or would I continue using my current, long, time-wasting route? If I am in my right mind and I am concerned with the amount of time I spend on the road, I would take the shorter route. I would save some time, giving me a moment to relax with my spirit and be thankful to be alive, living in a world of contentment with myself.

While I'm becoming aware of my inner man, my being, and my spirit, I make extra time to enjoy my relationship with it. I can vent to it, ask it questions, and receive answers from it (maybe not immediately, but always eventually). Sometimes we are not receptive to the answer our spirit gives us because it may not be what we want to hear. However, we can often avoid a lot of stress if we come to terms with ourselves by applying the Application and living with peace as our goal. Sometimes we have to say to ourselves, "No, I can't subject myself to that risk. It may jeopardize my peace, my freedom, my family, my sense of wellness, my happiness."

Happiness breeds life. Don't you just love to laugh? I can't think of anyone who does not like to laugh. It crosses all boundaries. It has one language, happy. How do you feel when you laugh? Think about it. The next time you laugh, think about how you are feeling. Try to hold on to that feeling for hours. Is there anything wrong with being happy all the time?

When I apply these tactics to my life, I feel free, clean, protected, powerful, and disciplined. If a risk stands on my path of learning, I will not avoid it. However, I do not take unnecessary risks, as they could cause me to stray from my path. Adversity is the weight of life. As we get stronger in our spirit, we can lift the weight and not be overwhelmed by it. The Spirit is a powerful source of energy, as will be discussed later.

According to Sigmund Freud, there is a vast array of brain space to be used. Using the Application allows you to come into awareness of that extra space and power. It allows you to become more sensitive to what is going on around you. You will be able to call on your intuitions with confidence, enjoying every moment you are alive.

I am very happy in my relationship with my spirit. I have acknowledged it and it has given me a new life that I previously didn't know could exist. A new life of power, freedom, and faith immeasurable, knowing that I have something no one can take away from me. This is something that helps me have more control. If ever in a compromising situation, I know my destiny gives me power over fear and over death. I live in victory. While I live, I can always share with others the power of my faith, and if I cease to be, I have victory on the other side because I know my spirit and it will recognize me when I leave this mortal grave.

Have you ever thought about the life of ants? They serve each other, work in teams, and protect each other for a common purpose. I wonder if they know how to cheat, lie, steal, or hate. If you have love and respect for life, then you will respect their life, whatever their capacity. All life becomes evident to you— the greens are greener, the wind has a different message, and your aura begins to show. Signs of renewal begin to show up in your face and you begin to look alive. No doubt, it's because you are now living instead of existing. You are controlling your atmosphere. You are where you need to be and you're happy.

I am not advocating being emotionless. What I am advocating is not allowing your emotions to control you. Closure is always good; finales are good too. These two entities give stability. When you have closure, you can move on. When closure is present, most likely nothing you could do would make a difference to the outcome. Whatever the situation, the end result will inevitably come out the same. Accepting closure can give you peace. It will help you to move on.

We live in a world of craziness, but you and I don't have to be a part of it. It all starts with you, me, and all who are willing to let go. Let go of judgments, ridicules, lies, resentments, and non-edifying conversations. Once you come in contact with the Spirit, it's very difficult to remain the same. It's a metamorphosis that cannot be avoided and a well-made decision to not attempt to avoid it.

I cannot explain the metamorphosis accurately in human words because the Spirit is above human nature. We have not gotten to it just yet. We operate in a closed system that gives us boundaries such as time, limited resources, and environmental setbacks such as rain, cold, and heat. We have to adjust to whatever our environment presents us. The Spirit has no rain, no heat, no hurt, and no pain. It is the epitome of freedom. It does not need a coat or a car and it knows no limitations. I can imagine the Spirit asking me, "Why did you do that? Why have you neglected your responsibilities?"

We all have something to do while we are alive. If your purpose is to find a cure for viruses, imagine the lives you would save. You would be saving lives long after you have passed on. Look at Sir Alexander Fleming, who used his life to find cures to preserve life. He discovered penicillin in 1928 and still to this day his discovery saves lives. What is it you can do with your new-found life? How can you use your life to become immortal?

Coming in contact with your spirit and allowing the fruits to operate within it will give you a song—a mission you will not be able to hold inside. Just like me now, I want to share all that I have gained with the use of my spiritual nature with everyone I can. I hope my message will improve someone's life. After you have completed reading this book, I hope you will examine your spirit and give it a chance to work in your life.

Sometimes we may have to get down deep with ourselves to achieve acknowledgment. There are negative forces that can throw us off course—thoughts of "I can't" and "this doesn't work." I don't believe in them. These negative forces and thoughts will render your efforts useless. You must believe in yourself. Acknowledge what is making you think. Do you think flesh thinks? Do you think your brain can function outside of your body? No, but the energy that gives it its ability can function forever. Ask anyone who has had an out-of-body experience. Ask her if she felt alive while outside of her body. She will tell you "yes" and that she felt more alive than ever before.

Acknowledgment, truth, forgiveness, and goodwill will help you to skim the surface of what it is like to live freely with the intuitive nature of the spirit working within you. If the Spirit speaks to you, listen. But what if you think the spirit tells you to go kill someone? Let's examine the fruits of the spirit: love, long-suffering, peacefulness, gentleness, kindness, protection, and preservation. Now would a spirit with this nature tell you to take the life of another? I think not. If you have voices in your head telling you to do harm to someone, you might want to consider the source. It will not be the Spirit of acknowledgment, truth, forgiveness, and love.

Ask yourself, "Is this love's nature?" What is love's nature? A physician gave me this definition of love and I agreed with him: *The unselfish will to do good to all of life, in all circumstances, under any condition.* That was very powerful for me and this is what I bring to you in the Application. Again, what is the Application?

•*Acknowledgment.* Accepting the spirit within you, opening up to it, speaking to it, allowing it to grow inside of you by applying the other entities of the Application.

•*Forgiveness.* Forgive yourself, forgive others, accept a clean slate, and start brand new. Say to yourself, "From this day forward, I Thee vow to not hold myself accountable for the past burdens I used to carry. I will allow them to wither and die. I am a new creature."

•*Truth.* I will start a new decisive moment. I will spew out of my mouth the truth, for I know the truth will set me free. It will preserve my new nature and will give me the peace I need to nurture my spirit. It gives me the chance to grow strong. For each truth is a step in the direction of peace.

•*Love.* I cannot say enough about love: the greatest, most powerful, enduring, patient, kind, gentle, warm, approachable, endowing condiment to life. It is the salt of living. Without it there is no life. The dictionary defines love as affection and closeness with a person. I identify love as the blood in my veins—irreplaceable. Love is power, love is life. Love is the most powerful force a person can possess. It has retaining power difficult to pull away from. Why would you want to anyway? Love is safe.

If you love me, will you purposely hurt me? Will you risk our relationship? Will you deny and resent me? I think not. Love does not do that. Mature love is love that has gone from giggles and affection to concern for the well-being of another person, causing one to lay down his life to save others. One who loves brings sight to the eyes of the blind? One who loves bestows knowledge and endures in spite of hardship.

Applying love to your life starts with truth and forgiveness. Once you are open with acknowledgment, you may then look for all the good things in everything you look at. If something is not pleasing to your eyes, look at it again. It is unique and different in its own right—the same right you have.

       ℁ • ℀

Beauty is in the eye of the beholder and we all have differing opinions as to what is beautiful. Right now I am giving an opinion of my firsthand experience going through the metamorphosis from flesh to spirit. It's wonderful, but somehow the word "wonderful" seems inadequate. I wish I could say a magic word and elevate myself to that realm, time after time—you know, cross back and forth. Wouldn't that be awesome? I know one day I will feel that elevation again and will remain in that nature.

There is no trick or magical potion to having a spiritual connection. All you have to do is really want one. Surely, you've heard of the "ask and you will receive as you believe" principle. Some of us have been blessed with the experience because we have rendered ourselves usable and available for the uplifting of humanity. We have been given the inner gift of having a formal introduction to the Spirit before dying, so we can share it with others.

We have been given eternal life. My gift of faith and spiritual endowment is so large I cannot contain it to myself. I want everyone to see it and enjoy it with me. I sometimes feel like I've been to a feast where there's plenty left to share. The feast continues to grow the more I speak of it and the greater it becomes, the more joy and peace I receive.

Are you interested in spiritual endowment? Are you interested in engendering your spirit? Will you acknowledge it? Our Father, Creator, and Author of our lives is love. We are saved by love. Our lives come with no long-term contract. Acknowledgment of this love will not turn you into a fanatical, overbearing, lunatic monster. You will have peace, understanding, and the power to say yes and no.

Okay, are you ready to get started? This will be the greatest gift you could ever give yourself, your children, and your loved ones. You will learn how to love better without discord. You will become long-suffering just as the Spirit has been while waiting for you to awaken and answer when it calls your name. If the Spirit says, "Get an umbrella today," grab the umbrella. If it says, "Take the long way home today," take it.

Obedience is better than sacrifice. What good will it do you to spend a whole hour or more a day sacrificing your time to read this book without at least trying to acknowledge the spirit within you? Why are you reading this? Simply because you were destined to do so and you have something else coming your way as the Spirit leads you to continue this journey.

You are headed for an experience of a lifetime—one that will give rise to your purpose in life. Appreciate yourself and your life. You are alive today along with other living spirits. It's as if your past life just melted away. You do not know where it went, nor do you care. It has gone away never to return again, for you have been made anew in the spirit of your mind. Whatsoever a man thinks he can be, he is, if only he believes in the power of love and the Spirit. For he can do all things through the Spirit who strengthens him.

ೞ 2 ೞ
Let Your Conscience
Be Your Guide

Have you ever talked to yourself as you went through the course of your day asking questions like, "Did I turn the stove off? Can I make this traffic light? Do we have milk at home?" By the way, who is "yourself"? Who or what is that voice inside your head that helps you to remember to grab your coat before leaving the house, make that phone call, and put gas in the car before going to work? Have you wondered to whom you were talking? When you make a choice, right or wrong, have you ever wondered what determined your decision? Do you still second-guess yourself, making costly mistakes in the process? If you've asked any of these questions, then read on.

You can avoid making costly mistakes, you can have greater peace in your life, and you can gain strength through obedience and application. If people would listen closer to themselves and weigh the consequences of all their decisions, relying on their spirit to bring peace in decision-making, they would make fewer mistakes, waste less time, and experience more peace. We all need direction in our lives and we have a helper. That helper is our spiritual self. Now if we study the Spirit and its level of existence and from where it comes, we can receive answers to those questions we ask ourselves.

Here's what *American Heritage Dictionary* gives as the definition for the word "spirit": *life-giving principle within a living being; the part of the human being associated with the mind and soul, distinguished from the physical body; the real significance of something; a supernatural being; strong loyalty and dedication*

The word "something" in that definition disturbed me somewhat because, in my opinion, it failed to acknowledge the Spirit. The Spirit is my Author, my Helper, my sense of wellness, my eternity. If I have an entity residing within me that is supernatural, loyal, and dedicated to giving me the principles of life, I think I could follow such an entity instead of having it follow me, while I struggle to make decisions and second-guess myself. "I started to do that. Something told me to take the long route. I should have gone with my first thought. I shoulda, woulda, coulda."

If we would only acknowledge the Spirit and give it the full attention and obedience it deserves, we would waste less time, forget things less often, and have more peace, greater faith, and a new way of living and viewing the world. Intuition abilities increase when you allow the Spirit to guide you.

So, how do you let your spirit guide you and how do you know if it's really your spirit guiding you?" Again, according to the abovementioned definition, the Spirit is loyal, dedicated, and most of all supernatural to our understanding. The Spirit will not hurt itself. The Spirit is your conscience. Your conscience is your inner man that prompts you to do well. It is aware of its environment, provides capable responses to this environment, is all knowing, and never sleeps.

Knowing this about my spirit—that it is my pre-server of life here and after—I am compelled to get to know it, communicate with it, develop a relationship with it, and allow it to be my guide. When I decided to listen to my first thoughts, my gut instincts, and be obedient to them in always, I received the clarity I needed in my life. I received peace, time, and, most of all, rest. I now recollect the passage in the Book of Matthew in the King James Bible that talks about giving up the yoke of life's troubles and the Spirit will make it easy. Give up your burdens to the Spirit and receive freedom from worry, stress, confusion, and turmoil. The Spirit will always tell you the truth, it will prompt you to be honest, and it will help you make the right turn. All you have to do is listen and become obedient.

There are a few simple exercises that can be done to not only test the spirit, but also your faith and obedience. The more you do them, the stronger your spirit will become and the more peace you will obtain along with wisdom and awareness. I don't know about you, but these are characteristics that I would like to have in my life. In fact, I do have them, I use them, and I am com-pelled to write about them. The Spirit gives me drive and will; it helps me to obtain a vision for my future and to focus to achieve that vision. The Spirit is not fiction, my friend. It is real and alive today in you. Let your con-science be your guide.

Our conscience is developed in our early days when we depend upon our parents to give us a sound upbring-ing. However, when this does not happen, as in my case,

19

we can still turn to our conscience, ask it questions, and make requests of it to live well and free of unwarranted burdens. Our conscience is our friend who will bear our entire burdens and guide us into the light of life. The liaison to the Spirit is the Application, as described in the first chapter. Using the Application in our daily lives and allowing the Spirit to speak to us and guide us, will ultimately provide direction toward our purpose for living, therefore giving us our prescription to destiny. We all can have a dream, vision, and direction in our lives if we just heed the instructor, the supernatural being who knows all about our existence and who will tell us about our existence if we just listen and obey.

The next time you hear the voice in your head telling you to gas up or take the long route, do it. In following the Spirit and communicating with it on a daily basis, you will come to know more about yourself. Sometimes when we discover ourselves, we want to change our lives to a less hectic, more advantageous lifestyle. This can happen now, today, if it means no longer living a lie. It is very important to be true to yourself, freeing up the Spirit to operate. The Spirit is good; it will not enter in where it is not wanted. It will not be intrusive; it has to be invited in. When I invited the Spirit into my life, I could not imagine inviting such influence in without cleaning up my mind. I had to empty it out and apply the entities of the Application, so that I would not suffer confusion by holding on to all the burdens that constantly kept me second-guessing myself, and ultimately delaying my spiritual growth. The Spirit wants to direct you; it will provide you with validity and acknowledgment.

This may seem far-fetched, but I have experienced it. I have tried the Spirit and it has never failed me. I have other friends and associates who have given up the blind life, have come out from the darkness, and are now living instead of surviving or existing. The infinite wisdom of the Spirit is there for you, has always been there, and will never leave.

What about the elderly people who have Alzheimer's? How can they achieve wisdom and renewed ability to function? They will once the yoke of burden is lifted and more often than not it will be lifted at death. Then they will be free again—free to have eternal life on the other side. This is why I stressed it would be more advantageous to teach the young discipline and how to achieve spiritual endowment at an early age, preventing them from living with burdens and dishonesty all of their lives.

Carrying burdens and having a conscience that carries hurt, disappointment, lies, and discord will tear the body down and cause reprobation. It will literally hinder the Spirit, because as mentioned earlier, the Spirit will not enter without an invitation and you really don't want to invite the Spirit to an unclean house. If you try to function with the Spirit in an unclean atmosphere, there will be war in your spirit as you fight back and forth with what is right and what is wrong. *Should I do it? Maybe not. I want to, but maybe I shouldn't. I wonder if? No! I'm doing it anyway.* You don't have to function this way.

Can you imagine the risk in such decision-making? This type of decision-making could cost you your life and for many it has. How about a new lease on life? How about a clearer understanding?

I want to live at the highest level I can obtain in this mortal life. There are people who do live at spiritual levels. It's a wonderful feeling. With God as the Author of life, He will not betray us when we rely on the helper He has given us since our life began. Once we are conceived and our lives take form, we have a spirit. And, we can achieve our destiny sooner and live within our destiny longer, when we learn to allow our conscience to be our guide.

If you think your conscience is telling you to cheat, steal, lie, hurt people, and do things that are evil and against nature, reconsider the source. Seek help from the Author of your life to free you from evil so that you can experience life in an abundant manner. All you have to do is want to change. A person not wanting to have a more abundant life is in reprobate and needs exposure to good at every turn of events in his or her life. The battle can be won. Evil cannot stand in the presence of good. What does the dark have to do with the light? Nothing! Nothing at all because even the tiniest beam of light will pierce the darkness and it will flee. Suddenly the eyes will adjust and you will be given sight. This is a great revelation. Not only is it great, it's free and available right here, right now. This is my prayer for you and me:

Father, Creator of all, give us the energy and intuition to hear the voice of the Spirit. Grant us a measure of faith to believe. Open our eyes to understanding. Instill in us the love that surpasses all things. Give us knowledge to know the difference. Help our spirit to grow. You are omnipotent. We belonged to you in the beginning and will in the end. Allow our lives to obtain freedom through accepting forgiveness and practicing truth. Spread your love over us and give our spirit and life a chance to know peace, understanding, faith, and goodwill. Allow the Spirit to speak now. Open our minds and hearts so we may have the life that You promise. A life of peace, love, understanding, and compassion. Give us a vision of ourselves with abundant life and the power to fulfill our vision.

ఐ • ಐ

Now I don't know about you, but I feel like if I prayed that prayer to my Father, he would deliver. I believe if I prayed that prayer to anyone who loves me and has the power to do it, he or she would also deliver. This is what love does for us. It grants needs and desires based on our will to ask. Ask and you shall receive. It's all true and amazing to say the least.

You may wonder how a person can become released in death. I have one word for you, Grace. Amazing grace, the gift of life—not earned but given—that will not be taken back. So you see, even in spite of denying yourself the chance for abundant life here on earth, in your demise your spirit is redeemed back to its Maker. Why not have a good life now, enjoying the fruits of love and obedience? Let others see your full life now, while you can testify about it, instead of using your obituary to validate your life.

Once the Spirit is working in your life, a sense of immortality may inhabit your being. This is the confidence you gain knowing you have eternal life. You are going to live one way or another, in this life or the afterlife. Make it count for something. Make your mark on the world by extending your wisdom to one who is less fortunate and hurting from disappointment and unfulfilled expectations. Help him or her to see that the best help is self-help.

Obedience is better than sacrificing two or three hours of praise, only to fall away 12 hours later. I would prefer to follow my spirit as it directs me, rather than to pretend for a few hours I have the Spirit. The Spirit is manifested in actions. The life of Jesus showed the manifestation of the Spirit. All those who were obedient sacrificed their lives to give humanity its vitality as we know it: Abraham, Isaac, Jacob, David, Solomon, David Walker, Sir Fleming, Sojourner Truth, Abraham Lincoln, Martin Luther King, Jr., and all those who devoted their lives to the betterment of humanity. Their spirits rested heavily upon them. They were obedient to the call and the mission placed in their hearts. Who wants to be next? Who wants to be the next great humanitarian for our misguided youth of today?

By no means am I telling you this is an easy road. Having inner peace doesn't mean you will not face evil or adversity. You will have to fight for others who aren't as strong or who haven't had the opportunity to meet someone like you to tell them about abundant life and peace. If you employ the Spirit in your mission, it will guide you and give you strength. The reward is not given to the swift, but to the one who endures to the end.

Let your conscience be your guide. Your conscience will not tell you to destroy yourself because it wants to lead you and prepare you for the eternal life. It wants to manifest itself in you so others can have an abundant life. It wants to make you an example of itself. Are you willing? Are you available? Do you want to live forever here on Earth and eternally? What more can a person ask for?

We all want the truth and we all want to live forever in good spirit, health, and will. I don't know about you, but I am happy. I'm happy you have read this far. I'm happy you may even consider inviting the Spirit in. I'm praying that in your darkest hour, the Spirit will bring you light, that you may see again, or for the first time. Go ahead! Give it a try!

Allowing the Spirit to guide you will indeed benefit you. You have nothing to lose but despair, mistakes, and disappointment. I have made mistakes, suffered, and often asked why. It's because I refused to listen to the Spirit. When I decided to listen, things changed. However, I do still make a few misjudgments and I know why I do. It's simply because I'm not listening. Listening is not an overnight thing. It takes practice. The more you practice, the easier it gets. So, how about starting today? What does your spirit tell you now? Do it!

Has your intuition ever told you that a certain person was untrue, could hurt you, or was trouble? Did you disregard the message and continue the relationship because the person was nice or you're too nice? More than likely this person will bring you trouble, directly or indirectly. Listen to your intuition and separate yourself for the sake of peace.

Although this may sound a little paranoid, we have to be spiritually watchful of whom we deal with on a daily basis. If we are to conduct ourselves in a spiritual manner, we have to deal with the spirit of the world. We cannot just deal with our spirit and flesh. We have to understand and deal with the spirit of the world around us and those we interact with in our daily lives. Who are they? Are they loving, kind, generous, tenderhearted, and humble? I believe this is the spirit we should instill in our young—the loving, kind, sensitive, and generous nature.

Being deceitful, backbiting, jealous-hearted, envious, and slanderous are the things that can kill a spirit and turn it into a reprobate. Again, allow your conscience to be your guide. Obedience helps you to help yourself.

ঞ 3 ଔ
Evidence

Please, Father, allow the content of my spirit
to rule my actions toward mankind and
I pray that spirit be of a loving nature.
—Terri D. McLennan

It was the day of my finals and I was failing. I had to make a very high score to pass the course and failing was simply out of the question. If I failed, I'd have to wait until the next semester or even an entire year before getting back into the class and I would be devastated. I needed the degree to get ahead in life and I prayed for it. Why would it be unreasonable for me to pass if I applied myself?

Well … to tell you the truth, I was in a bad situation. Just the stress alone from the circumstances could cause me to fail. I was dating a guy who was lying to me. I could feel it deep in my spirit. I was unable to think clearly while trying to discover why this person would lie to me, cover up things, and then say he loved me, even when given the opportunity to come clean. I was there trying to study and retain information while he would distract me with his lies. Lies like, "Yes dear, I paid the lease" (never revealing it was paid with a hot check). "My car was stolen" (when in fact it was repossessed). I could sense his uneasiness, but I didn't know how to confirm my suspiciousness.

Besides, I did not want to deal with his lies at the time. I had a final exam to pass to achieve my career objectives. I was almost going crazy. I knew deep down that I should ask this person to leave me alone and go away from my life. "Get him out of your space," my conscience would say. I toyed with this message for at least three more days. Meanwhile, exam day was drawing closer all the time. I studied the most when he was gone, at his make-believe job. I would suddenly lose concentration when he would arrive.

The spirit of a lie is strong and if you train your intuition, you can pick it up every time, like detectives do when determining whether a person is lying. Using this tactic and monitoring body language can bring lies to the forefront without the liar's awareness. My boyfriend could not understand how I knew he was not telling me the truth and my resulting apprehension. Therefore, he continued to play out his lies until he was caught with his hands in the cookie jar. Meanwhile, as I prayed to my Maker, petitioning for His help, the Spirit repeatedly told me to get that man out of my life.

I pondered the message until the day before the exam, which was at 10 o'clock the next morning. The voice became stronger and stronger. "Get him out of your life so you can concentrate and pass! His spirit of lies will hold you down. Let him go!" I finally spoke up. I announced that we needed to leave each other's lives and go separate ways. I could no longer live in the same space with him. He accommodated my request, of course, to save face, and walked out.

Suddenly there was a peace in my heart and I meditated on that spirit of peace. I took deep breaths of it within. I picked up my notes and began to study again. I was trying to remember the 12 cranial nerves and their functions, like which nerve controlled blinking eyes and pupil dilation. Pretty deep stuff, eh? Well, I did not need any pressure on me during this time. As I studied, I fell asleep.

When I awakened, it was 2:00 a.m. in the morning and I was very upset. I had flash cards all over my bed. I didn't know how much I had studied. I knew I needed to get a good night's rest before the test and I was really tripping now. I spoke to my spirit. "I hope I have done the right thing. I pray you are there with me during the test, giving me the intuition I need to mark the right answers for the questions. I need this and as an obedient person, I pray for the evidence of my good faith and trust in being obedient."

I closed my eyes and went back to sleep. The sun, shining through my blinds, woke me. It was 8:05 a.m. I rushed to my feet and I thought, "Damn it, the boys did not wake me as they usually do. I am going to be late." I had intended to get up about 6: 00 a.m. to look over my notes once more. Instead, I had to spend my time getting dressed and driving to school. I didn't even have time for a light breakfast. I got in the car, warmed it up for a few minutes, popped a mint in my mouth, and drove to the school. They say if you pop a mint, it will open your sinuses, allowing you to breathe better and think more clearly because more oxygen reaches the brain.

I talked to my spirit the whole way, gaining confidence, building faith, and speaking victory over my life. Whether I passed or not, I would accept what the Spirit had for me and I believed it loved me, wanted to protect me, and would give me the desires of my heart, if I acknowledged its guidance. I knew I would receive the fruit of my labor. I walked in, took the seat I was directed to, and began my test. I wavered not on my first choice of answers on the test. I prayed hard for understanding.

When the test was over, I left. It had been announced earlier that the results would be posted by 4:00 p.m. that day. This score would determine whether I'd move into the next semester. I was riding a thin line and I needed a high score to pass. I walked away with confidence and said to myself, "Oh well. That's it." I decided to go home and sleep away the pain.

When I got home, I felt comfortable. Instead of going to sleep, I addressed my mail and messed around on the computer a while. Before I knew it, my boys were walking in from school. I told them I wanted them to go with me to the school to see if I passed. I was very nervous, but I kept my head up. When I arrived at the posting board and located the last four digits of my social, I discovered that I received a score of 81—exactly what I needed to pass!

We were allowed to view our test if we wanted to, so I looked at mine. The questions I missed were few and were ones that I did not have a reference to draw upon— information I could not recall because it had not been applied anywhere in my mind. Nevertheless, the bottom line was that I passed the course and was able to move on because I listened to the voice telling me to remove the negative forces in my life.

I needed to have a free mind to think, learn, and apply myself without interference. Some people just aren't productive with the person they are with. It's important to maximize the stability in your life so you can see the evidence of your labor and obedience. Often our blessings are clouded by the troubles of another, preventing us from enjoying our own blessings because we are too caught up in the burdens of another. As always, misery loves company.

Evidence shows up when we are obedient to the direction of our spirit. Surely a nature of love and self-devotion would not turn on itself. The nature of evil manifests itself in lies, cheating, stealing, selfishness, and jealousy. All of these evils can find a home in the darkness of your soul, but if you allow the light to come in, it will defend against its ground, causing the evils to flee. Darkness cannot remain in the presence of light—light that eyes cannot see.

New intuitions, reality, visions, knowledge, increased awareness, and spiritual growth are manifestations of using the Spirit as a guide. I cannot imagine not wanting these intellectual abilities. What is so good about them? You do not need a college education to develop these senses. All you need is the ability to think about your mortality and what threatens your soul. Learning this at an early age will help a young person become a thinking, compassionate, intuitive person who does not give his fate to chance. No haphazard living, as we'll discuss later

Learning how to see evidence comes from practicing obedience. It's not an easy skill to master, at first, but develops and becomes more on target with regular exercise. Remember that it is a baby. If you have not been obedient to your spirit before, your relationship with it is still fresh and you have to learn to trust it. You have to honor the direction it gives you. If you allow it to grow, it will reward you with evidence of your labor.

Evidence is asking for what you want and applying yourself toward that purpose. Nothing worth gaining falls into your lap. It takes work; however there are some miracles at work. If you're not waiting for a miracle to fall into your lap and can dedicate yourself to the improvement of your natural given abilities, the evidence of your labor in raising your awareness to your environment is just an intuition away.

So, how do you know if you're making the right choices? If you're making the right choices, you'll first of all get the desired results. You'll also have peace about the results, you'll be ready to accept the fate of your actions, and you will have hope for the best.

You will make mistakes sometimes because you have not applied your senses enough. More often than not, we are well into our 40's or even 50's before we come into greater senses because we have gone through the process a number of times over the years. We say to our children that we've been there and done that. If we teach our children to listen, they will not have to experience the long route as we did. Teach them mental telepathy like my parents did. I did not have to be spoken to in church. All I needed was *that* look, which said a thousand words.

We can teach our children to learn to use their senses in a non-threatening manner. However, teach what is logical and listen to the voice in your head for direction. It is as simple as guiding your senses to tell you what is right for that given moment. When I would ask my sons to do certain chores, they would ask me how to do them.

I allowed them to perform their chores the way their minds instructed them. As a starting point, I showed or explained to them what the end result should look like after finishing a specific task. Once they completed a task to their ability, I pointed out all the correct and incorrect areas, leaving them with a mental image for future reference on how to get a job done. This process is called learning.

For example, taking out the trash. What procedure would you go through? What is logical in your mind? When we take out the trash, no one has to tell us to take it outside. We see the dumpster or trash container outside. We don't take it to the bathroom and pour it down the toilet, which would not even be logical to a 5-year-old.

We should study the Spirit just like we study other things in life. Let's not dismiss the teaching of the Spirit in our lives. Not just for adults who have had trials, learning about the Spirit allows us to learn from others' mistakes. Avoid accidents by watching as others who choose not to listen make mistakes.

Evidence is a powerful gift because it gives us strength to continue our growth processes. At the outset, we may fail a few times, but with sincerity, truth, and faith within, we will not continue to fail. We will develop intuition about our environment and those who are in it.

I've had associates that did not have my best interest at heart, and because of their nature and mine, I felt like I was carrying their burdens too. There were times I would feel their spirit of jealousy and contempt for me. I would ignore them and tell myself that they couldn't hurt me, but in reality, the negative energy from those spirits detracted from my joy and was not edifying. I separated myself from those spirits because they brought me down. I learned to keep certain personal information to myself, away from the mind of a dark spirit.

Have you ever lent something to someone only to receive it back damaged or broken (or lost), after lettin him or her handle it? Has anyone ever stared dead at you while you were eating, causing you to drop your food?

Do this exercise. Stare at the back of someone you know and concentrate on him or her. Call his or her name in your mind. Observe how long it will take them to turn around and look at you. That use of your telepathy and spiritual strength can grow into strong abilities to help you determine your environment and the spirit of others. Who can judge the Spirit but the Spirit itself? Who can see the Spirit? Only the Spirit can. The Spirit is communicating with you all the time. It will see you through. You will not be disappointed if only you have faith and patience with yourself. If you commit to listening and obedience, your life will change drastically and immediately.

Once practicing and operating in the Spirit, you will begin to feel the power of your inner man, your spirit. The Spirit is meek and gentle, not boastful or pretentious. The Spirit is yours to rely on in a humble manner. Boasting about your ability to read a person's mind and abusing that ability will almost always throw you off track, simply because that's not the nature of the Spirit. Evidence is a personal matter. It's between you and your spirit. Evidence is not to be exploited or provoked because it's the nature of the Spirit and Earth. Evidence is a personal experience.

If I were to tell people that I communicate with my spirit and what it tells me, they would probably think I was crazy. However, I am not crazy, but rather spiritually self-driven. Driven enough to write this to you and caring enough to share it. Your spirit is like your heart, which you're not going to expose to harm for fear of getting hurt, damaged, or hardened.

We all have at one point or another been exposed to a hardened personality—someone who is very negative, rude, and heartless. Do not cast your pearls before swine, for they will trample all over them. When you have evidence of an intuitive thought, it is a good thing to reward yourself for recognizing it and to thank the Spirit for allowing you to perceive it. Know that you are in connection with the Spirit and the evidence will continue to reveal itself. Practice does not necessarily make perfect in this case, but it helps the spirit and soul to grow and will give you the evidence needed to use this power to guide you through.

Can you imagine how much more informed and wiser you would be now if you started this process at age 10? I started giving my sons this knowledge when they were in their teens, and I explained to them about the evidence of their awareness and intuitiveness. I wanted them to know that when using this ability, they actually have a connection with a higher power, a connection of power given at birth. How does a child know to cry for his needs? How does he know to listen and learn to talk? He taps into the intuitiveness of his surroundings and his mother has a special bond with him (or should I say intuition?) that allows her to anticipate the needs of her child.

The Spirit does the same for us—it anticipates, warns, and informs us of all things, if only we listen and receive our evidence. We have telltale signs of impending events. Disease gives us warning before it actually sets in, but do we listen to it? Most often we don't.

Ninety-nine percent of the time, an impending cardiac arrest will give at least 2 weeks notice. Most individuals will ignore or deny the symptoms and wait until they are supine or in such pain that they can no longer bear it. Unfortunately, by then, it is often too late. What do they receive for their negligence? Evidence of what was going on all along.

What about the silent killer hypertension, a disease most people don't know they have? Well, most people do not monitor their blood pressure. They may see a blood pressure machine at the grocery store, think for a second to take their blood pressure, and then deny their intuitive spiritual guidance saying, "Nah, I'm pretty healthy. I don't have time. It doesn't run in my family. It's mainly an African-American disease." They end up not taking their blood pressure only to soon find out that they have hypertension. Just as the Spirit can warn you of imminent danger, it can warn you of other things that are about to take place and will give you evidence of its prompting, be it good or bad.

I enjoy seeing the evidence of my intuitions. I will listen most of the time and when I do not listen, I am praying all the way for protection. I stay in communication with the Spirit. Today, my spirit prompts me to have a family talk and prayer. If I ignore it, I feel like I will lose my direction or my sons will be exposed to a traumatic situation. If we ask, we will receive; if we plan, we will have direction; if we have direction, we have purpose. Finding your purpose gives you reason and evidence for your life.

Do you ever wonder why you are alive? Why did you make it when others didn't? I am very interested in why I live. When I find out about others who didn't make it, I look at my life and realize that I'm here for a reason—a reason that stretches beyond biological ones. The next time your spirit speaks to you and prompts you to do something, listen and look for the evidence of your obedience. If you are lucky enough to be given intuitive thought or information for someone else, share it gently with him or her, just as the Spirit gave it to you. Then you can observe your evidence.

A few years back, I had a pregnant classmate who everyone said was carrying her child as if it were a boy. When she was only two months pregnant, I told her she would have a girl. I just felt like she would, which was my intuitive nature at work. The Spirit also told me to tell her that this baby would be very different from her other two children. Most of her other friends were persistent saying, "Oh, I bet it's a boy. It looks like a boy." Later, when she had her sonogram, she was informed that the baby was a girl, which was evidence of the intuition I was given for her.

It felt good when she told me. And, no, no, no, there wasn't any bragging, boasting, or I-told-you-so's. I just congratulated her on her findings. In return, she told me, "You are the only one who told me I was having a girl." I simply smiled to myself and told her my spirit told me it was a girl.

That kind of evidence is irreplaceable for joy in knowing you are connected to the Spirit and receiving its fruit. Many of us go to church for most of our lives and hear the Word, but rarely are we told how to live in that Word. We're only told what's going to happen if we don't abide in that Word. I was tired of hearing about a God who loved me so much, yet he was ready to allow Satan to kill me if I didn't abide in His Word. Yet, no one told me how to abide by the Word.

Then one day, I woke up and wanted to know how to access my spirit and how to know if I was doing it right. Well, I was given a taste of the Spirit and I heard Its voice. I listened and received my meat of the word. Now, I know how to abide by the word and I have evidence of my obedience.

You too can obtain the evidence you need to listen and abide in the Spirit. Revelations of the Bible tells us: "Those who have ears to hear, listen to what the Spirit has to say and abide in that." It's important to listen, watch, and communicate. Ask for your direction on a daily basis. Everyday is a new opportunity to achieve a new level of understanding and evidence. When you wake each day, speak to your spirit and ask for direction.

Humble yourself to listen to your spirit and know that what you receive is truth coupled with compassion for your soul. Ask and you shall receive. Have faith that what you ask for is being delivered as you speak. Have no apprehensions or doubts. Trust in the Spirit with all your heart and lean on it. It will give you evidence of your request.

At times when I have problems, I pray and ask for my direction and my help. Usually I will say, "Hmmm … I'm having problems. Something good is about to happen. This principality I'm dealing with is here to vex my spirit and make me feel as though I'm not loved, protected, or being directed. I know better, though, and I laugh it right out of my life. I do not worry about anything that cannot change my spirit or stop me from breathing.

The things that darken my spirit are the things I pray about. I just give them up. Why? Well, first of all, it's not my fight to begin with. Second, there are principalities that try to beset us. The Spirit is my shepherd who watches with close vigilance to guide and give me evidence of its presence so that I can feel safe, protected, and loved. I learned long ago not to trust or depend on anyone else for guidance, except my Helper, who I know is there to help me always. I am the evidence of its validity

If you connect with the Spirit, you will have evidence in your life. You will begin to enjoy its direction, the security of knowing that it is always with you, and the intuition you will receive. You will have evidence to support your intuitions. You won't have to say, "I started to go that way" or "something told me this would happen," because you'll be listening to your spirit.

Even if nothing happens, that's a good thing. It's better to have nothing happen than to have something you can't control happen that will cause you despair or disappointment. If the Spirit tells me to take the long route, I will take the long route. I may make it to my destination on time or a few minutes later. On the other hand, I may have avoided traffic delays or an accident, or I may just simply enjoy a more peaceful drive. Again, listen to your spirit and receive your evidence.

℘ 4 ℬ
Detachment

Be ye separate from the world, for you are not of this world
and it does not recognize you.
Therefore, what it does not recognize, it seeks to destroy.
—Terri D. McLennan

I was daydreaming so intensely, I was actually there in my dream. I had detached myself from my environment and I could no longer feel. I was completely in another world. In that world, I had no pain, no fear, no worries, and no concerns for my environment. I was more in tune with where I was, which was in another environment away from the boundaries of the flesh.

Detachment is a good thing if done with the proper perspective. You don't want to be detached if you're learning; you want to be in tune with what you're about to learn. Detachment is beneficial when you are in a situation that you cannot do anything about. When you are hurting, it's good to detach. When you are giving advice or direction and need to remain unbiased, it's good to detach. I try to avoid giving advice to someone I am close to because, undoubtedly, I will give the wrong message due to my emotional attachment to that person.

When you are detached, you can see. You are able to stand on the outside, look inside, and see the picture clearly. When you love someone, you see them through rose-colored glasses and give them the benefit of the doubt. When you are not emotionally involved, you see everything. You see all the imperfections and all the faults and bad habits. This is why detachment is good if you can achieve it in critical situations.

We all have watched as family members fall into emotional entrapment with individuals that we say are not good for them. We hear about battered women who stay with their abusers, don't press charges, and remain in the situation because they love them. These women believe their abuser will change if given enough time. They love them enough to give them that time, not realizing that the behavior will not change without help. When the abusers do change, it usually means a change of relationships as well. Meanwhile, the women are being destroyed in the process.

We on the outside, detached from the conditions, can see clearly. This is why detachment is good. When I was a young girl, I watched as injustices were imposed upon me and wondered what to do. In that wondering, I learned to detach from the environment so it would not hurt so much. I acted as if these injustices were not happening to me. Since there was nothing I could do about it, my spirit would protect me by detaching me from the scenario, thus giving me the ability to forgive and move on.

Somehow, through all the adversity, my heart has not been hardened. I still can forgive and move on. I do not carry grudges. I do have hurts I deal with, but not on a level that they affect my ability to function in a rational manner. I still trust, I still love, and I still give chances.

I learned how to analyze things while I was detached. I assessed the conditions and the situations. I would say, "Obviously, he doesn't know what he's doing; otherwise, he would not do this to me." I would wonder why I didn't feel violated. I didn't simply because I wasn't involved spiritually. I was detached. I was on the outside looking at my body and the person imposing the pain. I watched the anger in the person's eyes, took the abuse, and absorbed the hurt like a sponge. Once it was over, I was exhausted, but I was free.

I am not saying that I do not hurt physically. I do have physical pain in some cases. For the most part, I want that protection from my spirit. We need the Spirit to protect us from the things that can cause us harm. Some issues and attitudes that block the Spirit are hatred, jealousy, enviousness, coveting, lies, and cheating. These things will cause the Spirit to regress because it functions best in a truthful, natural environment. However, detachment is a way to separate spiritually from these hurts, and it will help you to develop compassion for others.

Would you purposely hurt a loving, meek, and defenseless person? Could you, in your spiritual mind, hurt a child who could not protect herself? Could you be hateful, jealous, and abusive? I don't think so! Most individuals act out negatively due to illness and prior hurts. When you are on the outside, you can see the evils and the illnesses that afflict a person. With this vision, you gain compassion for him. This does not mean you condone or ignore the behavior. However, you can have compassion for him or her and you do what it takes to help, even if it means reporting him or her to the authorities, forcing him or her to get help through acknowledgment of his or her injustice. If he or she has to go to prison, so be it. The bottom line is that the individual has a chance to recover and correct improper behavior.

Some people call it tough love when we push our children out of the nest. Doing so does not have to be a vengeful matter; it is standing for what is right and giving notice that you will not tolerate certain behavior. It does not mean that you love them less; it means you care enough to help your children correct their negative behavior. The time may not be the time they would choose to be corrected, but who chooses the time of his or her correction? Correction is usually forced upon a person for improper behavior before he or she acknowledges it. We play until we are caught; then, once caught, we want to change. If we could detach ourselves from the improper behaviors of others, we could free our emotions from hurt, thereby maintaining an optimal environment for spiritual development.

People ask me, "Are you ever embarrassed?" Most of the time I answer no because I don't live a life to be ashamed of. I detach myself from issues that bring about embarrassment. From all those ill-conceived words that can lower a person's esteem, I move away. I think the only time I'm embarrassed is when I'm on the golf course and I completely miss the ball. Even then, it's just a game and why should it have a right to affect me? The only way it affects me is by making me laugh. I detach because nothing and no one has the right to affect the confidence that my Author, my Father, has given me. I am pleased with my spirit and the condition of my heart.

I will not allow anything to change them, except for the Spirit itself.

How does a person detach? Detachment comes through meditation. Once you begin to meditate, you can coach yourself to enter a reality where you're looking down at you body. Close your eyes and visualize your body in the position it is in. Visualize your body in a still, motionless state View it as a shell because you are not in there; you're on the outside looking at the shell. In that shell lies all the physical feelings of embarrassment, hurt, anger, hatred, pain, disappointment, and all the other negative feelings we experience on a daily basis. You see, the Spirit is not bound by and has no concept of these things. It doesn't hurt, it doesn't feel pain, and it has no bondage to time or space because it doesn't live within those boundaries. It is eternally free, immortal, and away from human nature

Detachment can be done at any appropriate time and is part of recognizing your spirit. Being in the Spirit is being detached from worldly matters and communicating with ourselves. When we pray, we try to detach from our surroundings to feel the love of God and to feel secure in our prayer. I do not know anyone who prays and watches TV at the same time or prays and reads at the same time. I know people who pray and drive—often a short prayer or conversation. They keep their eyes open and look straight ahead, yet still focus on their prayer.

Being in traffic is not always the best time to pray or meditate, because to feel the Spirit, we want to close our eyes in a quiet environment, seek out the Spirit, and talk to It. However, God is unlimited and He can hear us everywhere. All we have to do is talk to him in sincerity

A person has to develop the ability to detach, which becomes easier with practice. The process of detachment starts with assessing your situation and then taking yourself out of it. Analyze the people involved and put yourself in their shoes—just for a moment—to determine why they are doing whatever they are doing and why to you. Try to come up with solutions regarding how you would have handled the same situation should the roles had been reversed. Build a shield of faith around yourself. Acknowledge the Spirit and tell yourself, "This is not happening to me. No weapon formed against me shall prosper."

Remember the old childhood saying "Sticks and stones may break my bones, but words will never hurt me"? That's detachment—never let spoken words hurt you, since they are merely someone's opinion. You are your greatest fan. Some might say this is a form of denial, but it really isn't because you're not denying the situation, you are merely assessing it and deciding not to become attached to it.

You can say "no" to the situation as well. In thinking yourself well, you can say "no" to ill feelings and replace them with "I feel good and I will continue to feel good. I'm strong. I am healthy," and so on and so forth. Never speak negatively about yourself and don 't allow others to do so either.

I can remember times when I was younger that I'd go out, drink alcohol, and get tipsy. When the time came to go home, I would detach from that "tipsy" feeling, not allowing it to rule me. I would simply gather my senses, do what I had to do to get home, and then thank God that I always made it.

Another method for detaching is assessing yourself in the mirror. Talk to yourself. Look at your hair, eyes, face, teeth, and as much as you can see. Look at yourself as if you were looking at someone else, then speak. Ask yourself what you want in life. Ask yourself if you are happy. In fact, this would be a good time to unload all your problems and questions. But don't forget, the most important factor in this exercise is truth—being true to yourself.

I remember when my sisters would come to me and unload all of their problems about relationships, loves, bills, and whatever. I would get fed up because they would unload everything and then go back for more of what they just unloaded. I started telling them to go to the mirror, unload, and ask themselves if they wanted to continue to take more junk around with them. By unloading on yourself, you'll eventually get fed up with the situation too and do something about it.

Mirror talk is good. It can help you detach. When you talk to yourself, your spirit is talking to your flesh. I usually look in the mirror and say, "Look at you. Are you happy?" I can go to the mirror and say all the things I wanted to say to others, but didn't. I can make decisions there with my spirit being my guide. I can cry, laugh, and evaluate situations there in privacy, and can do whatever the Spirit tells me.

The next way to detach is to sit quietly in a chair with your feet flat (no shoes) or lie flat on your back with your arms stretched wide open. Then, become aware of every part of your body, from the top of your head to the bottom of your feet. Look up at the ceiling, close your eyes, and imagine yourself getting up while looking at yourself on the floor. Look at all of yourself. Now that you are detached and in your spirit form, feel that form, recognize it, and allow it to take you places. Be careful, though, because you could fall asleep.

The best place to go is someplace within your everyday environment: the kitchen, bathroom, bedroom, etc. Take a moment to look out the windows. Enjoy being detached from your body as it lies on the floor. Remember to make sure that the place is quiet and that you won't have any intruders. It's very difficult to detach, especially the first time, when the TV's going and there are external noises.

After you become proficient in detachment, you can go into your room alone and become detached, while others are around, if you just want to get away. Think of a place you would like to visit. You can even create a place in your mind, a place of serenity and peace. You can go there whenever you want. It can be your place of detachment. It's all for your peace, comfort, and the release of burdens that you carry.

When you return to your fleshly body, make sure you have let go of some of the things that beset you and leave them out there. Once when I detached, I took hurt, pain, disappointment, animosity, and certain individuals outside of my spiritual realm and left them there, then went on to my serene world and enjoyed my peace and lightness. When I returned to my body, I didn't bring any of those negative feelings or individuals back with me. I left them there and was able to experience the fruit of my detachment. I was no longer carrying those negative people or things with me; therefore, they could no longer influence my personality or spirit.

We are supposed to learn from our mistakes; however, sometimes we go through the same things again and again. Each time, the issues present themselves from a slightly different angle with a new hurt or disappointment. That's why it's important to assess each situation, ask questions, and detach yourself. If the situation hurt you the first time, it will hurt you the second time. Although it may take you a little longer to find that out, the bottom line is the same

Learn to make smart choices according to what you, and only you, want. If you go around doing what other people want and denying yourself, you will not end up happy, but selfless. Learn to love you, and accept only what you need and want. This will allow room for growth and there will be less junk in your junkyard.

Save yourself from unnecessary pain and anguish. It is not selfish to do what you like. Selfishness is being self-serving at the expense of others. When you cannot share or extend yourself, you will not be able to give to others. It's not selfish to not give of yourself because someone else wants you to. You have to give because you want to give. That's what makes giving worth doing—wanting to do it.

I have found it better to not give my word so freely because I am bound by my word. I have always heard that a person is only as good as his word. If I give my word, I am bound by it. When making a commitment I will say "maybe" or "I will try," unless I know without a shadow of a doubt that I can honor my word. This saves me from the guilt of not keeping my word and reduces the number of things that I have to take to the detachment dumping ground.

Some may fear detachment because they think they may not come back and die out there. However, it is not the flesh that runs the body, but the Spirit. The Spirit lives on and on and on. You will return to your shell and feel great after returning. You will probably not be the same person because in profound experiences, we are changed. It is difficult to get into the Spirit and remain the same as before.

If we know better, we do better. That is, when we know the difference, we do not continue to operate in a nonproductive manner. If you know a better route, that is the route you take. You don't go out of your way to avoid convenience. No, you embrace it and use it to the best of your ability. It saves time, effort, and frees you up for more of the things you like to do. Detachment will give you a better understanding of your life and others. It will also give you the opportunity to free yourself of disappointments, anger, emotional distress, and help you make better decisions about certain things. You have to try it to see how it works in your situation.

I have talked to many people who have used detachment as a tool in their lives. In several cases, after detaching, they would visit loved ones who were on their minds; soon they'd discover that these loved ones needed them and had been calling out for them. Similarly, have you ever phoned someone who said, "I was just thinking about you"? Happens all the time. It is the Spirit connecting the two of you together, causing one to contact the other. There are times when we need to see someone miles away. By detaching, we can go visit with him. In a later conversation, he may say, "I had a dream about you the other night." He'll probably think you are out of your mind if you say you were there, because he has yet to experience detachment himself.

Mentally and spiritually, I once summoned a companion by being very persistent, focusing on his name, and pleading with his spirit to call me. I was over 200 miles away and needed to talk to him. Within minutes of my request, he called me, simply because our spirits had connected and he was obedient to the call. If you have someone emphatically on your mind, do not resist the call of your intuition, because more than likely, she needs or wants to talk to you or you need to see her. Get in touch with her. If you know where she is, you can go visit her.

You may wonder, how can I go to see her if I don't know where she is? What if she is lost? Under these circumstances, you will have to call on the Higher Spirit, God, to guide you to her. Just because you can go into the spirit of your mind, does not mean you are all knowing. You are knowledgeable of what you instill in your spirit. You have to get your understanding from God and He will give it to you. Just ask, be sincere, and have faith. Trust that God knows everything.

As I was writing this book, I discovered that I really needed the inspiration of the Spirit. Most of the time, I would receive a revelation from Above and have a yearning to write before I could actually sit down and record my thoughts. My information would come in the form of spiritual intuition. As I prayed in the Spirit, the Holy Spirit would inspire me to write. I would feel detached from my surroundings and everything going on around me and I could sit and write for hours without consciousness of time, space, or the environment. It could be too cold or too hot inside the house, but I would not be aware of it until I was finished, back in my body.

Detachment is a good thing in its proper time and place. It is not a random thing unless controlled by God, and even then, it's not random, but His will. When I would see an awful car accident or a traumatic event take a life, I would always wonder where that person was spiritually. I always believed that God removed the person's spirit from his body prior to the event and only the lifeless body had to absorb the trauma, not the person himself. He was taken from this life, moments before the accident or traumatic event. It seemed so much more acceptable to believe that the individual was set free before the accident or event. I found this way of thinking helpful, so I used it in the analysis of the death of my own son, who died tragically. I believe God removed his spirit from his body ahead of the events that we as humans associate with the cause of his death.

We will live beyond the human existence. I just wish that all those who have had an out-of-body experience could make those who have not had one understand that concept. When you practice detachment, you are not dead from your human nature, but rather merely taking a break from it. You can go back at will. However, when the Master of your spirit calls you or removes you from your human nature, you are finished with your human appointment and you are changed in the twinkling of an eye into a complete spiritual being. You will not be able to return to the body at will.

Did you not know that your life is not your own? However, your way of living *is* your choice. The Author of your life has control over your life on Earth, its beginning and ending. You can, however, choose how you live with the Spirit. Just like I have power (or at least think I have) over when I will finish this chapter. You have the power to make choices whether you want to abide in the Spirit or the flesh. You will not be able to do both. Once you learn to detach, you will like it, as does everyone who has this ability. You will choose the Spirit over the flesh because it is so much nicer than the flesh nature and there are no boundaries in the Spirit to where you can go. No, you do not walk there; you appear there, wherever you have allowed yourself to go. You will feel exceptional when you are able to accomplish detachment and will do it repeatedly to gain the peace and serenity you feel once in that state. The Spirit is stronger than the flesh. It's the Spirit that is life. The flesh has no power.

Detachment is special and I would encourage you to try it repeatedly. If you're not successful the first time, that's okay, just don't give up. Make your environment a place where detachment can happen. Pray for it. If you want it badly enough, you can have it. Ask your spirit to guide you into a place of peace and exploration within your soul. This is a procedure that needs to be practiced over and over again, so do not feel disappointed if you do not get it the first time. If you have not done this before, you will have to remember your spirit is young. Like a baby, it needs to grow and you will grow with it. Then you will be able to receive the fullness of its nature. It is love in its purest form.

Here's a true story of a little girl whose father died when she was living with foster parents, away from her mother. She was only eight years old and had heard her foster parents talking about a little girl who recently died of an illness. Until then, she had been under the impression that one had to be old to die and she had heard that when one dies, he or she goes to be with God.

When she overheard that this little girl had died at age 12, she had mixed feelings. At first she was afraid of the thought of a young person dying. But, as she thought more about it, it seemed more and more acceptable and even preferable to her.

Since she was not with her mother and father, she thought to herself, "Why not be with God?" She knew He loved her and it was peaceful with Him. Maybe she would meet the little girl who died and they could be friends up there in Heaven. So the more she contemplated, the more she wanted to go be with God. She made up her mind and decided she was ready to go be with God too. With this decision, she went out into the front yard, stood in the middle of the green grass, and slowly descended to her knees. As she looked up into the sky, it was a beautiful spring day. The weather was perfect and the sky was blue with clouds floating across. It was warm and the grass seemed lusher and greener than usual. It seemed liked the perfect day to die and go be with God. The little girl, down on her knees, began to pray:

Dear Lord,

I don't like it here anymore. I would like to come and live with you and the little girl who died last night. People here are mean. They lie to each other, steal, fight, and kill each other.

My father is there with you and I don't like it here anymore. I would like to come where you are. My mother is not with me anymore, and I just don't like it here. Can I come and be with you? I would like to go tonight. When I go to bed tonight, will You come and get me and let me be there with you, my father, and that little girl?

ഏ • ൦�

After saying her prayer she got up from her knees with all confidence that she was going to be with God tomorrow. She played the rest of the day and was so happy. She told no one of her secret. It was just between her and God. Besides, she figured they would know when she was dead the next morning that she had gone to be with God and it would be okay. Soon it was bedtime. She put on her best gown, kissed everyone goodnight, said her prayers, and got into bed. She could hardly sleep, like the night before Christmas or a birthday party, because she was so excited about going to live with God.

Eventually, she did doze off to sleep, only to awaken the next morning in the same bed she was in the night before. The same people were around her. She was still alive, as she was the day before; however, she was not as happy. She was very disappointed, sad, and did not know what exactly to think or do. As her day progressed, she thought to herself, "I guess I have to wait until I'm old to die."

She also came to believe that she would always live and never die and that God would watch over her. With this conclusion, she learned to detach from the world and live in the Spirit. She could experience Heaven whenever she wanted. She could feel God with her all the time, protecting her from all the liars, thieves, and murderers. She would have conversations with God all the time and He allowed her father to visit her, telling her that things were going to be all right.

She gained confidence and spiritual strength. She used the mechanism of detachment when she was hurting or being mistreated. She would leave and go be with God until the emotional or physical trauma in her life was over, then she would come back. When she returned, she had a forgiving heart and a loving nature.

She decided she was going to be a nurse when she grew up, so she could help people heal and be good to each other. Maybe she would even teach them how to detach from their world of turmoil like she does, so they would not have a wounded heart like those who steal, kill, fight, and hurt others.

I was that little girl and I still long for that day when God will say it's time to come on home now.

Detachment is a good thing. Try it. Who knows, you may find your destiny and the purpose for your life.

ഇ 5 ൨
Growing Through The Pain

No pain, no gain!

Pain is a sensory perception arising from tissue damage. Sometimes we will classify an emotional disappointment as painful, such as the loss of a loved one. However, it's actually anguish, not pain, that has us in disarray. Anguish is all emotional and provided for our growth. Usually when something hurts us deeply, we will not venture into that realm again for fear of experiencing the hurt or pain again. Therefore, we have a valuable lesson before us, and if we accept that lesson, then we have gained knowledge.

In order to grow, we must go through the fire. When we go through the fire, we grow. I call it "fire" because learning is like fire. It is self-sustaining and produces light. When we learn, we are able to sustain ourselves in this world and we are able to see as if a light has been turned on. We then gain enthusiasm for life, others, and ourselves. If we ask for our understanding, we will get it and we will grow. However, our trial is by fire. We have to go through that rapid chemical reaction—the change of life (and I'm not talking about menopause or the midlife crisis). I am talking about the change from flesh to spirit.

It is a painful process. We lose those who we thought were our friends. Situations arise to detour us from our original goals. Individuals offering peace, love, and happiness will appear in our lives only to eventually prove to be detours filled with pain and disappointment.

There are many avenues to growth and sometimes we have to take all of them until we are fully aware of all the wiles of evil and deception. The first step to growth is to lean on the Spirit for understanding and to trust no man here on Earth, because 99¾ percent of the time, man will let you down. It does not matter who he or she is or what he or she does. He or she will eventually let you down. We are human and we are fallible.

Trusting in God will set you free and save your friendships too, because you won't lose emotional trust, since you never gave it in the beginning. What you can do is hope for the best instead. Give your best as a person without expectation. Disappointment means unfulfilled expectation. Without expectation, there is no disappointment.

As I mentioned earlier, growth is a really painful process; however, when we come out of it, it will prove to be well worth our efforts and we will be happy that we did. It's almost like listening to our parents, which is the hardest thing, because we all know our parents don't know anything. Yeah right! Parents know a lot if they have lived and experienced what they know. When I was about 18, I made a conscious decision to just listen to what my parent had to say and to follow. When I did, it proved to be a very fruitful thing and well worth the effort.

Many times I would say to my own children, "I cannot say this enough ..." and then they would try to guess what I was about to say. They usually guessed correctly because I had said whatever I was saying so many times before. When I tell them something and they disobey, it usually comes back to haunt them. I just pray that one day they will wake up, truly listen, and learn how to consult the Spirit for help with issues.

I have lost a son to disobedience. I ask why all the time. "Lord, why did you take my child?" He was 18 years old and lost his life hanging around with the wrong crowd, a crowd that did not value life. He was at risk and of course thought, "Parents don't know anything." It didn't matter what I told him about the people he hung around. I could not choose his friends for him. That mistake of disobedience cost him his life. I am at peace because I prayed that the Lord would take him in His arms and protect him; and He did. I will never have to worry about him again for I know he is safe with my Father.

My middle son is now going through the same process of learning to listen. God has protected him on more than one occasion. He has direct evidence. Once when I went out of town and left him alone in the house, I instructed him to go to school and work and told him not to hang out with anyone who could get him into trouble. He didn't obey me and guess what happened? He now has a tragedy to live with for the rest of his life—all due to disobedience. Had he listened to me and abided by what I asked of him, things could have been different. His friend might still be alive and he would not have this tragedy creeping into his thoughts or experience nightmares about his loss.

You see, we don't have to be at risk. All we have to do is listen to what the Spirit has to say and listen to our parents who love us and try to give us direction. Listening is not an easy task, but when we do it, we grow. It is a painful thing to give up our own understanding; however, when we do, we will grow. Even the King James Version of the Bible tells us not to lean on our own understanding, but rather listen to the Spirit and what God has to say.

How do you know it is God talking? Consult your inner feelings. You know how you feel when you do something wrong, and you know the peace you feel when you are doing things right. It is the same principle. Principles are powerful tools to use in our lives. Principles are inarguable standards that can shape the heart of man. They help us to treat others like we wish to be treated. If I treat you with respect and love, I would love to have that in return. If I were to consciously treat you manipulatively, would I like to be treated likewise?

I had a friend tell me that a con artist didn't mind being conned. In fact, he said, the artist would take pleasure in it. I find that difficult to believe because he is in the business of conning, not being conned, and no one likes to be beaten at his own game. I think I would be insulted if I was a con artist and was conned at my own game. I believe I would go away and reassess my motives. Nevertheless, we have these individuals in the world to help teach us lessons and there is a lesson even for the con man.

We all grow from pain and we should learn from our mistakes. Oftentimes, we may have to go through the same lesson a few times or some tragedy has to take place before we actually wake up, but we will finally learn. As a young adult, it took me several abusive relationships to learn how to choose my associations. I am currently a single parent, which is best for me right now, because I can get to know myself, my standards, and what I really want in a mate. I am dependent on God for my guidance and I am not consumed. My mind is free to pray, write, love, and do, as I will. I do not have the issues of relationships in my life now and I feel good. I can hold out until the right person comes along who can feel my spirit and I can feel his. The right person is someone with whom I can share a partnership and a relationship with God.

It took time to dispose of the baggage, years of garbage and hurt, I had from old relationships. Now I am free to wait and I am free to love. I lived in an abusive relationship for the first 14 years of my life as an adult. All I wanted was for someone to love me and not hurt me. If a man said he loved me, I devoted myself to making a relationship with him. Then, after a short time, when I discovered he really didn't love me, I would deny him by cutting him off from my affection. Ultimately, he would hurt me for revenge.

This cycle would go on for a while until I prayed for understanding and asked, "Why Lord?" My answers came and I gained peace from within. I had to go through the fire of learning and listening. I had to learn to love me. I had to set principles and standards and I had to know my spirit. Once I gained knowledge of my spirit, I would no longer accept less than what I wanted out of a relationship. God is still working in me and giving me this time to have vision, learn, and breathe.

In Heaven, we have no weaknesses and do not require a partnership. The Spirit has no gender. We have a friendship with God Himself and we don't need another person to validate us. As humans we are co-dependent. We do need each other while we are here on Earth living the American Dream, going to college, getting married, buying a house on the hill, having children, working until retirement, and dying.

I myself am not a traditional American Dream success story. I have had many adverse experiences due to my lack of knowledge. The hard road of fire I have walked has molded me into a spirit-filled individual. I have had to rely on the Spirit to shape me into the person I am today. I can now help others who are not living the American Dream and going through the same hardships I went through. I can show them that no matter what route we go through in life, we all end up needing grace to protect us and the Spirit to guide us. The sooner we learn to listen and pray for our understanding, convictions, and obedience, the less we may have to suffer. The hotter the fire, the stronger the lesson.

You have seen individuals who have been crippled from gunshots due to gang-related incidents. Many of these individuals are now telling others, who are headed in the same direction, that the gang life just isn't worth it. The lesson these former gangbangers learned was what it took for them to listen; however, had they listened to their parents or whoever told them to stop their violent activity, they might still be walking.

If I had listened to my peers sooner, I may not have ha to go through those abusive relationships. Nevertheless, those trials helped me grow; although they were painful, I still learned. I learned to listen, pray, and depend on the

Spirit to guide me. When I started listening to the Spirit, I was ready to abide by it and be obedient to it. After we learn to listen to those we can see, those who give us sound advice that proves to be fruitful, then we can use that same principle to listen to the Spirit, allowing it to direct us to what is right fo us.

As I grew up, I was a blessed child and I always knew God would use me ever since He left me here after that day I prayed to go be with Him and He did not take me. I knew He had a purpose for me. I always wanted to fulfill that purpose My childhood home was tormented by dysfunction and discord, arguments, fights, hurts, and disappointments. Enduring all these things helped to mold me into a loving being.

I could have grown bitter and harbored anger in my heart because of the way I had been treated, but there was another plan for my life. I grew in grace as I went through the pain. I did not allow the hurt to tarnish my faith, or at least God did not allow the hurts to tarnish my heart. He spare me and gave me a chance. He changed me because I asked Him to save me from the power of hurt. He opened my eyes and showed me the other side of this life. I could not accept it right away but as I grew, I received my strength and knowledge. Now I am attempting to share what I have learned with you.

I hope these words are inspirational enough for you to want to develop a relationship with your spirit and the Author of your life. If we could remove expectations and all the other beliefs that rob us of a relationship with our spirit, we could gain our sight and understanding. It is a difficult process, but we have to be willing to go through the fire. No matter what you go through or how much it hurts, never give it to anger or hatred. Don't allow it to make your future dysfunctional.

Always tell yourself you are going to make things better for yourself and do so with the help of the Spirit. If you wait on someone to improve your life for you, you will be waiting for a long time. For example, if he or she does something that doesn't turn out as you wish, you'll be ready to blame him or her for your unhappiness. Ultimately, however, you are responsible for your happiness, not someone else. You have to make the correct choices to facilitate a happy life. If you place the responsibility for your happiness in someone else, you put yourself at risk for sorrow and hurt. Really, your happiness should be in knowing your destiny and where you are going in life. Let no one steer you off course. Create your own destiny.

Know what you want in life and accept nothing less, as long as it doesn't cost the life of another or exploit others. You cannot go through life mistreating others in your pursuit of happiness and think that your joy will last. Life is a cycle. Whatever you do comes back to you—magnified. If your happiness lies in material wealth, then you are in for more disappointment.

Again, your happiness should be in knowing your destiny and your relationship with God. Knowing who you are in this world and allowing yourself to be used by the will of God will give you tremendous growth into the future of your life. It will give you immeasurable understanding and you will be knowledgeable well beyond your years.

We have advanced in society for over a hundred years and have improved everything from sight to sound. We can see around the world on the Internet, yet we cannot get along with each other. The advancement of society has been at a standstill for over 30 years. Substantial improvements have not been made since Martin Luther King, Jr., and Far-rakhan, who brought a million people together to help them learn how to support family values and principles. Today, we need someone to lead the way. We need another Moses, another Sojourner Truth, or another man, woman, or child who will take up the staff of truth to unify society

We are all the same in spirit; there is no gender barrier. We are now living as if we are in a capsule, ready to grow into a spiritual being when we trade places with the flesh and this carnal world. In the Spirit we have no barriers of time or space. We are everywhere. We see all things. We don't see colors. We have only one race, one gender, and one type of being—a spiritual being—just as we are now human beings in the flesh who have a spiritual inner being. We need to make our spiritual being part of our social being by touching one another's spirit rather than just greeting each other in the flesh.

Driving along the road one day, I thought about pre-monitions I would have about people and recalled an inci-dent from early in my nursing career. I was working in oncology and had a patient dying of cancer who was terse, mean, and demanding. As a result, no one wanted to care for her. I had the pleasure of taking care of this patient one night. She was rude to me and I was disgusted with her. Her room was at the end of the long hall and she would constantly call for help. Back in that day, we didn't have intercoms, so I had to walk down that long hall at least 20 times just for her. And having eight other patients to care for made my job difficult … very difficult. This patient was eventually discharged, only to return a few days later.

On the day of her return, I had a vivid dream about her. She was sitting up in bed, was pleasant, and looked pretty. I enjoyed taking care of her and she was sweet to me. That evening, upon arriving at work and receiving my assignment, I learned that this bitter cancer patient had returned and that she would again be placed under my care. I thought, oh no! Then I remembered the dream I had about her, which I shared with my coworkers, who informed me that the patient was not sitting up in bed, nor was she nice. However, she was again at the end of the hall

I knew I was in for another night of hell at work. When I went to her room to make my initial patient assessment, I realized that she was in grave condition. She was calm and peaceful and welcomed my presence; she was dying. In fact, she died about two hours after I arrived at her side

As I continued driving along the road, it dawned on me that I had the power way back then—over twenty years ago—to see into the lives of others, a gift given to me by the Spirit because I cared about people. I was able to see my patient free of disease and carnal bondage, as she is now in the spirit. She is nice, friendly, and free of disease and hurt. That is how I saw her in my dream. I saw her life before she was able to see it. I gave her hope when I touched her as I cared for her. She was able to transcend into spirit with faith.

Recently, another patient came into the ER where I was working. He was blind from diabetes, crippled from a stroke, and was in severe pain. I asked him while caring for him, "Do you want to be free?" He said "yes," so I grabbed his hand and I prayed for his pain and suffering to stop, with him in agreement. After caring for him, I transferred him to an intensive care unit. Just an hour later, he transcended to the other side, free from the bondage of disease and bodily pain. He had no family with him; he was alone. I let him know it was okay to embrace the Spirit.

As we grow, we can all see people as I have been blessed to see them. It took me 20 years to realize this gift. Imagine what I could be doing now if I had discovered this gift years ago or had been taught this discipline years ago by my parents. After 20 years of figuring it out, I am still thankful that at least I got it. Now, I want to spend the next 20 years helping others develop the gift. We need to grow. Sure, growth is painful. However, you will not die from growth, but you may die if you do not grow.

As I write this, I sense that someone or maybe a few will not understand this. Nevertheless, as time goes on, everyone who wishes to grow will grow. The process may take a little longer to manifest within some hearts and minds but with persistence it will happen. Planting seeds for the mind and heart to receive the Spirit is major work. Just like it takes the right soil to grow the right plant, we must plant the right seed for the right person.

In our society, evil forces work over time with high principalities of deception to force conformity to the American Dream. All these different religions and attitudes exist to separate us; however, in the end, we find ourselves united as one entity. We can grow into that unified entity now by fostering spiritual growth within our society. We can plant seeds of love, respect, and unity without barriers. Just like the trees live in harmony with Mother Earth, the grass, and the water, we don't see one tree fighting with the other. No, trees grow and are nurtured side by side in the same Earth soil that can nurture us, if we allow ourselves to grow in it.

Enjoy the freshness of the foliage. Allow the breeze of the desert to warm your bodies when you need it. Allow the herbs and vegetables to nurture your health and growth. There is a life of health, wealth, and happiness out there. We just have to re-establish our values. All you have to do is take a simple test. Write down the things that you do to facilitate health, happiness, and wealth in your life. Then among all the things, choose what is most important to you. What can you do to give yourself happiness, health, and wealth? You may have to define what health, happiness, and wealth mean to you. For example, what is wealth? For me, wealth is the value of love in my life and my character. My health, of course, is a direct result of how well I take care of my body to avoid disease and harm. My happiness is in knowing my destiny, the Author of my life, and my position with Him.

It is important for us to have a relationship with our spirit, so we can operate in it daily. Knowing who we are in relation to this world, our families, and each other is another step toward our spiritual growth. As we move into the next part of this divine enlightenment, we can learn who we are and what we represent in this world. Who knows? When you grow up, you may be the next Moses, Sojourner Truth, Abe Lincoln, or Gandhi—someone who will make a change in the lives of others by bringing our world closer together in love.

ജ 6 ന
Do You Know Who You Are?

When you look in the mirror do you like what you see?

When you think of who you are in life, do you think of what you do for a living? Do you think of yourself as a mom, dad, sister, or brother? When you look in the mirror, what do you see? Do you love what you see or are you constantly trying to change what you see on the outside with makeup, different hairstyles, or weight loss?

Why not think of yourself in terms of your spiritual being? Are you able to recognize your spirit? Do you know what your spirit means to you, your family, your mate, and the world? Do you know why you are alive? What is the most unselfish thing you've ever done? Mark those things down and read them all. Do they tell you anything? Can you compare your life with any of the men or women of Biblical days? Are you a Judas, Paul, Job, David, Ruth, or Jezebel?

Do you know who the Author of your life is? Is it you or our Creator? Do you know what your purpose is for living?

In this chapter, you will learn to recognize your spirit and the purpose of your existence. All you have to do is think about your life and how you live it. Are you the source of your family's pain or gain? What is your primary motivation in life? What drives you everyday to do what you do? Are you caught up in survival, doing what is necessary to maintain your current standard of living for yourself and family? Are you doing something for mankind? Are you driven by the desire to leave behind a legacy to the world?

We should examine ourselves on a daily, and sometimes hourly, basis to determine what our everyday actions and verbalizations mean. How many half-truths did you speak today? Did you help anyone today? Did you boast or lie? Did you take something that did not belong to you—be it a pen, some tape, a lighter, or any object that wasn't specifically given to you or that you didn't purchase. Did you speak in a manner to someone today that was not edifying? Did you hurt someone today out of selfishness? Did you pray for understanding? In the King James Version of the Bible, Paul talks about examining ourselves to see if we are operating in good faith. In 2 Corinthians, he encourages us to prove ourselves to see if we really know ourselves. Are we making our own choices or are we bound by tradition and habit?

This is the perfect time to examine yourself and your life to see what you have left behind. Do you do things for outside recognition? We all should be motivated by love, concern, the spirit of our minds, and what is good. Say to yourself, "Whatever is good is what I will do."

Now, let's take a look at what you are doing. You know that you are alive for good reasons, right? Okay, examine all that you've done to help or hurt mankind. Compare your actions to a mission, function, or task. If your mission has not been a good one so far, why not start now? Good, you're ready. All your motivations should be spiritually led and governed by goodness, and love, not by selfishness and the pursuit of recognition.

Would you like to do something for the world? Would you like to be the next Moses, a Sojourner Truth, a Norman Vincent Peale, or another Oprah? Do you qualify? All you have to do is ask yourself. Remember, he who sows sparingly reaps sparingly. Be happy with whatever you choose to do. Do it because you're happy to do it and because your loving Author is watching.

As I write this book, I am totally inspired. I can't sit and just write at will. I require a revelation of knowledge and a clear message of truth. I know that my truth may not be truth to everyone, but it may touch someone's life and help that person. Applying the methods here will enrich lives if done in sincerity.

When I listen to my spirit, it tells me what to do, say, or write. Meditation and prayer allow the Spirit to guide me. When It compels me to get up and start writing, I go to my computer or notepad and I write. Usually, whatever I've written sounds edifying and inspires me to share that information with others. These revelations need to be documented for all of us. Our days can be so full of distractions that we lose sight of our prophetic thoughts. It's very important for me to record my thoughts as they are given to me.

When I am obedient to the Spirit, I feel good. My reward is inner peace, one of the fruits of the Spirit. It has allowed me to know myself and God, for He is the one who drives me daily and He uses me because I am available for His purpose. God sent all the other prophets—and even me—to give us a message of goodwill toward men and love for each other. "Thank you, Father for seeing enough in me to use me to help others."

Would you like to be available for a good purpose? Are you filled with goodwill? Does your light shine? Does your spirit prevail? To find your purpose, you should search deep within your heart to discover from where your love flows. What is the best thing you could do to help others and be happy? Could you be charitable to someone's life? Not necessarily with money, but with love and whatever the Spirit guides you to give to that person. Be sure that what you do is not of a selfish motive, but rather for goodwill guided by the Spirit.

Our Creator always uses people to get his message across. Are you available for your purpose in life? Can you be a Martin Luther King, Jr.? A Harriet Tubman? An Abraham Lincoln? These individuals gave their lives for the betterment of others.

As a nurse for over twenty years, my work is a mission and a practice. This career is not my job; it is my mission in life. I take care of sick individuals because I love helping and giving my services in love and compassion. Daily, I am compelled to do my best, to give encouragement, and to look beyond patients' personalities to respond to their needs, like giving a drink of water to someone who can't get one himself. Although I may go through changes in my mortal life, I am still available for God's use. I have been blessed and I know it. I feel it, eat it, sleep it, and drink it.

Now is your chance to examine your spirit to find out what it has been waiting for you to do. Are you living the life intended for you? Who are you to your family, friends, and the world? What type of sister, brother, mother, father, or employee are you? Do you extend your knowledge to your family or employer? Will you be renewed in the spirit of your mind to fulfill your purpose? Will you examine your life and consider your purpose? Can you start fresh right now and give love to someone who needs it? Can you be a light to someone in the darkness? Can you help? Will you?

The previous questions may help you to learn a lot about yourself. Your heart's intention will tell you about your spirit and how it is motivated. It can be motivated by love or discord. We all have a conscience—with the exception of the mentally ill—and, in at least some part of our heart, love exists. It won't be very difficult for you to find out who you really are to those in your life, and it's up to you to determine if you need to modify any behaviors.

Remember, in order to live free and feel your spirit nature, it is extremely important to be true to yourself and others. Truth equals freedom, peace, and happiness. To live free, you have to be willing to share with others and be a part of making others happy. Use the questions as an opportunity to get rid of old baggage and learn about yourself.

Once, years ago, I went on a self-cleansing spree. I went to my sisters, my mother, my husband, and all those whom I may have treated indifferently and prayed and asked for forgiveness. It was at that very moment I was forgiven and I felt clean. I went and humiliated myself before my family in an attempt to get rid of guilt, not realizing I was born forgiven. My life was paid for today, tomorrow, and forever. This is what knowing my destiny tells me. However, it also helps us to ask for forgiveness because doing so will always make us feel better.

You too can know your destiny. And after you've finished this book and have decided to follow its lead to the spiritual realm, you will begin to know your destiny. As I come across books about how to become closer to our inner man and spiritual realm, I wonder what difference my book will make in readers' lives. It's really very simple: just try these processes, apply them to your life, and give them some time to work for you. They will work if you're consistent and honest.

As you allow this phenomenon to work, you will experience growth. It may be painful, initially, because you will learn many things that you weren't aware of and perhaps didn't want to become aware of. You may have to hurt other people to be true to yourself. But being honest with yourself, others, and the world is all part of the growth process to achieve freedom. You will become the person you were born to be. No more pretending, no more role-playing. Just you, me, them, and all of us free.

One evening, I believe it was mid-March, I went out wearing a pair of white slacks. As I overheard a lady talking about how it was not the right season to wear white, I thought to myself, "Self, we're not in bondage to these traditions of what, when, and where. We are spiritual and have no boundaries. We can do what we want, when we want, and it doesn't matter who cares. First of all, we have found our destiny and what we do will support that destiny. We are living our life's purpose, so fashion and fads do not affect us. We don't care about fashion trends, but we want to look good, inside and out, as a symbol of good personal care. However, it doesn't matter if someone else likes our appearance or not." Saying and believing something like this will help you to know yourself.

I challenged a friend, who was very conservative, quiet, and subdued, to spruce up his life. He had always wondered why he could never find a proper mate, yet he consistently looked for women at nightclubs and around his old neighborhood. I told him that if he wanted to find a nice, educated, confident woman, he needed to stop selling himself short and look around the college campus, the library, and other places where this type of woman would likely be found.

My friend didn't think he was good enough for this type of woman, even though he was a professional, owned his home and car, had everything else a bachelor could want, and was really a great guy. Obviously, he didn't see himself as he truly was. He didn't see his value in life and what he had done to make himself a good man that any good woman would love to have. He was honest, professional, a homebody, great looking, and a good provider. He had every reason to think a lot of himself. He just needed to be true to himself by stepping outside of the inferiority box to discover who he really was.

Discover your self-worth and your worth to those you love. If you were to introduce yourself to someone, how would you do it? Would your introduction be, "Hi, my name is Terri. I'm a nurse, mother, and student"? No, I think not. For me it would be, "Hi, my name is Terri. If they ask what I do then I say, "I'm a mother. I am spiritual, honest, straightforward, sometimes humorous, single, and the last-born child in my family." I will not allow my job to identify me even though it's my mission. I am not my job, nor my job me. Usually, when I'm socializing, I don't tell people I'm a nurse for various reasons.

I'm not ashamed of my life's work. My work has its place and it is very special to me, so I keep it special so as to not exploit it or myself. The things that make me who I am are my likes and dislikes, my preferences, my attitude, my body language, and the type of communication that comes out of my mouth.

So, what's your position with your family, your friends, your associates, and the world around you? Who are you really? I am my Father's child, doing His will for my life. I'm the one who philosophies and uses logic in my immediate family. I'm the nerd who goes to college who has dreams of a better life. I'm the one who always tell the truth. I'm the one who prays and avoids altercations. I'm the preacher in the family. Some of my family members think I'm arrogant. Some say I'm a know-it-all or that I'm too serious. Some just don't know who I am because they don't know me. They know of me.

You will see a different world when you begin to renew yourself. Some people will find themselves wanting to be single or celibate. Some will really want to settle down. Others will have to break hearts or accept that they are homosexual. Some will have to retract lies. As you renew yourself, you'll discard all the junk that inhibits your freedom and stops you from being yourself, allowing you to discover your place in the world around you.

When you realize who you are and decide to be true to yourself, you can start walking through some doors, doors to your future.

ஐ 7 ര
Doors

A means of approach or access
An entranceway
A way of passage

In our society, our lives are programmed for us until the age of 18, or even 21. During that time, we go through various stages as planned. Some kids excel and go ahead of others, but nonetheless formal education is mandatory. So, we advance through the levels, walk through these doors of maturation and preparation, and go on to opportunity. Some doors of opportunity or adventure we pass by for fear of the unknown or unfamiliar.

When we reach the age of decision-making, we have the option to choose which doors we enter. Unfortunately, upon reaching the age of decision, some of us don't have a clue as to what constitutes a good opportunity or what is useless. If we don't know ourselves, how can we make the appropriate life or career choices? How do we know these doors aren't detours? (We will talk about detours in a later chapter.)

When you decide to walk through a particular door in your life, are you sure you're headed for the right destination? Are you doing something mama (or daddy) wanted you to do? Are you embarking on your childhood dream? Are you about to become what you've always wanted to be as far back as you can remember? Are you following the traditions of your family instead of following your heart's desire to be a rig driver, teacher, or author of books?

It's sad to give your life to many years of study and commitment to end up hating what you do. Doors are beneficial if you choose the right ones. How do you know which door is the right door? Ask the spirit inside of you for guidance. Ask it what you really like about yourself and what you can do to make a living that you will not only enjoy but will also allow you to achieve your desired lifestyle.

Choose the door that represents what you want for your future. Working as a nurse for many years, I've seen medical interns come and go through the hospital—most of them young men and women trying to finish their residency so they can begin a private practice. I would ask myself why I didn't become a doctor instead of a nurse, since the position seems so much more rewarding. Then I'd sit back and think about what I was doing when I was the age of these interns. Why did I choose nursing instead of medicine? It was because my self-esteem was low, I had no support, I thought it was too expensive, and I believed that I could not pass the entrance exam for med school.

We choose doors based on how we feel about ourselves. Therefore, we must develop our self-esteem at an early age to be confident visionaries for our future. That is what this book is all about—finding your destiny as early as possible so that you can enjoy your life longer. If I was as confident in my youth as I am now, I probably would have chosen to go to medical school instead of nursing school. Now don't get me wrong, nursing school has been very rewarding for me for more than 20 years. However, now that I can see my full potential as an older, more mature person, I intend to achieve my Ph.D.

When I was 12 years old, my foster parents asked me what I wanted to be when I grew up. I said either a nurse or a teacher. As I got older, my teenage life revealed the likelihood of my becoming a single welfare mother. However, all that changed because I remembered my dream. At 20 years old with a 2-year-old son, I was working in a neighborhood store for a little bit above minimum wage and still living with my foster parent. I wanted more out of life and never forgot my dream of becoming a nurse.

One day while thinking about my life, I asked myself the proverbial question, "What do you want to do with yourself and what options do you have?" I had no college money, no car, and plenty of responsibility. I just couldn't stop working. Who would take care of my son? No one for free. Pondering how I could change my life, I prayed about it, which was very important. Then, out of the blue—or correctly stated, my prayers were answered—certain people were placed in my path. I got a letter from the Social Security Administration informing me that they owed me $2,400.00 for back pay from my father's death. The money was a blessing, allowing me to buy an old car, a '69 Pontiac LeMans.

Unexpectedly, one of my obstacles had been overcome. Next I had to figure out a way to go to college? I

decided to join the Air Force. I took the tests and quali-
fied so well, in fact, that they wanted me for the Intelli-
gence Department. I knew this opportunity would give
me the chance to make a decent living to take care of my
son.

When I told my foster parent what I had done, she
told me about a new program mentioned in the newspa-
per, the CETA program. The program had been started
by the Carter Administration for displaced homemakers
and welfare recipients to help them get out of the welfare
system and start careers. When I signed up for CETA and
indicated that I wanted to go to nursing school, they
asked me if I had applied to the school of my choice. I
drew a blank as I had no idea how to apply or do anything in that regard. CETA, however, explained the
application process to me.

So, I went to the nearby college and applied for RN
and LPN classes; both required testing, which required
money—money I didn't have. Again, another person
was placed in my path, a lady from the office of CETA,
who told me CETA would pay for the testing. All I had to
do was sign up for the exams and CETA would let me
know when and where I could take them, so I did. After
taking the exams and all my pavement pounding, things
were quiet for a while. Wondering what would happen
next, I became impatient, so I went back to see the Air
Force recruiter, who was scheduling a day for me to be
sworn into the military. As that day approached, I
resolved within myself, "I guess this is it, the right door
for me to go through."

On my way out to get sworn in to the Air Force, I met
the mailman at the door. In the mail was a letter from the
college stating, "Congratulations, you have been

accepted into the nursing program." I was so excited that I never went to the swearing in ceremony.

Walking through that nursing school door has now sustained my life for over 20 years. I was 21 years old, earning twice the money of my parents and friends. I had furthered my education and surrounded myself with those who could help me continue the lifestyle I had chosen for myself. Some may say that the chances of all the things that happened in my life to make nursing school a reality are extremely unlikely and reserved only for a select few, but I say not true. All a person has to do is move in the direction of what he wants to do in this life. If you're scared or intimidated by a particular set of doors open to you, then create other options for yourself, or as we sometimes call them, plans "b," "c," etc.

It is important to teach our children how to make choices and plan at an early age, so they can look forward to a long, rewarding life. The more you like your life, the more you'll like others and be able to have a peaceful, compassionate life. As children we should learn to set up options for ourselves, create doors to walk through, and make plans. Just like we teach our children common nursery rhymes, we can also open their eyes to what people do everyday by instilling them with questions such as, "What will you do as an adult?"

We should encourage our children to use insight when making their choices, helping them to truly grow up. Life doesn't have to be haphazard anymore. Your life can be your dream. You can direct your life, instead of allowing life to direct you with bills and circumstances. We can speak to our lives, people! Did you know that if you tell yourself what you want and remain persistent, your desire will come to pass?

Your energies can be directed. Just like if you tell yourself you're sick, you'll feel sick, you can also tell yourself you're well and you'll be well! If you tell yourself that you're going to have *that*, whatever *that* maybe, you will have it, provided you move i *that* direction. For every action, there is a reaction. Therefore, you must act to get the reaction you desire. If you want to go to college, you don't go to the local bar to get started—you go to the college campus. If you just go to look around and visualize yourself as one of the many students you see there, that is a start. You have just erected a door, an option. All you have to do now is refine that option and create a vision of the benefits of walking through that door.

Then you can go on to other possibilities for your life. Build more doors. Doors are great. Doors give us confidence because "where one won't work, the other will," an old saying from the South. Choices give us confidence, unlike putting all our eggs in one basket. Build more than one door on your house. Make some windows too, so you can look out into your future and visualize another 5-10 years of what you want to do in your life.

With each door comes *responsibility* responsibility to yourself to continue walking through the door and advancing on the path of that doorway. Don't erect a door, only to not walk through it to the reward beyond it. What should you do if you go through a door you really didn't want? Suppose you really wanted to go through another door, that wasn't available at the time when you had to make a choice Because I'm bold, like having many choices for my future, and want to do everything possible in my life, I would take the door I initially wanted, as long as it wouldn't hurt anyone in the process or require me to break my word

We should create doors so we can have options in life. Options and doors are signs of success. Part of success is achieved when people seek you, instead of your having to seek them. Careful thinking, weighing outcomes, and looking at the benefits and drawbacks of each door you build will allow you to make a change or go to another door with confidence.

Some doors are big, heavy cast-iron doors, like those leading to a relationship. These doors carry a whole lot of weight and aren't like the doors you build for your career. Doors that come with a lifetime responsibility are marriage and children. When you go through these doors, hopefully you will have already been through some of the lighter ones. The doors of marriage have now become lighter because of the ease of divorce. However, when you reproduce with your mate, you create another life that will live on, even after divorce. This child, a product of you both, creates a relationship between the two of you that will endure for all of your life and your mate's. It's very important to be careful when walking through a relationship door, because these doors are much heavier than others.

Friendship doors are also heavy. These doors are critical too, because you want to choose your friends wisely. Friends are supposed to be benefits in life, little perks along the way. They are like cookies; they can stay with you in more than one way. If there's a person in your life who's not a benefit to you so you can be a benefit to him or her, then this person is probably an enemy. He or she will throw negative energy in your path, so it's best to avoid him or her.

Jealousy is a real killer of productivity for both the person with the jealous feelings and the person toward whom the jealousy is directed. Jealousy creates bad karma or energy that conflicts with positivity. When jealousy is present, energy is wasted in conflict, so avoid people who harbor jealous feelings toward you so that you can maintain positive energy.

There is more to life than doing all the routine daily activities of living such as waking up each morning, performing personal hygiene, going to school or work, coming home, having dinner, watching TV, and going to bed. Oh how boring! Take that same scenario and make it more profitable and enjoyable such as arise at 5 a.m.; work out for 30 minutes; shower for 15 minutes; pamper yourself with lotions and other emollients. Look in the mirror and ask yourself, "Am I happy today?" and say "yes." Have a breakfast at 6 a.m.; 6:30 a.m., get dressed for work; 7:00 a.m., leave for work if you have to drive in rush-hour traffic; otherwise, take a peek at the morning world news.

In other words, plan every moment of your day. You may think that sounds like something a 40-year-old would do and you're right! But it's not going to take you 40 years to do the things it took others 40 years to develop into, right? The benefit of learning from others' mirrored doors is that you'll learn faster and can reap the benefits of this knowledge sooner, allowing you to enjoy life longer.

It's a big pill to swallow, but success doesn't come without effort. Doors don't open without effort. We need to make our own way. We must establish ourselves. Doors allow us to do that by defining who we are to ourselves, our families, and to the world around us. When someone asks us to elaborate about ourselves, we should always begin by discussing who we are to ourselves. For example, "My name is …. I'm smart, usually friendly, and a parent. I like to read and my favorite color is yellow." These statements define who *you* are, not your job or your education. After you're able to tell others who you are, then you should tell them about your education or profession.

It's all about you—your doors, your life, and knowing yourself early in life to enjoy more of it. Move forward in life and spend less time in decision-making and going through the process of trial and error. I like doors because if I go through one, I'm growing and I know what opportunities stand behind them. I have had to go through some difficult situations in order to grow; however, had my childhood examples been different, perhaps I would have become a doctor earlier in life. Instead, I walked through the heavy doors first because of my environment and neediness.

With the information in this book, you can make more informed decisions about your life. In this life of doors and passageways there are many avenues to travel. The most important choice is the door that will sustain you and help you to continue to grow. We have to know who we are before we can be anything to anyone else. We have to remember that it is our responsibility to ourselves to further our lives past our parents' instructions. It's all about you and what you want to be in this life. What we do for others when we visualize our dreams will help to propel us toward our dreams. Sometimes a smile and a thank you are sufficient.

Do not allow anyone or anything to get in your way on your road to success. You have to be willing to step out on faith and believe in yourself. You should not be letting yourself down, especially if others are letting you down. It is your responsibility to be good to yourself. After you have built doors for yourself, and walked through those doors, and achieved your goals, then it's time to help others. This is the reward of success.

To be able to inspire others, even beyond your own dreams to greatness, is truly a most significant mission. If you are a governor, then inspire someone else to be president. Just like the Olympic torch passing from one person to another across the world, to continue our journey we must also pass on inspiration and motivation. Ah, the doors of life are many! It's the door you build that will take you into your productive future. It doesn't matter what your current situation is. Although it may look hopeless, you can achieve your goals if you really want to. Build a door for what you want, put your ducks in a row, and pick 'em off one by one. Advance through that door in your life and become the person you really want to be.

It's time to keep your head up, eyes open, ears tuned, and spirit ready because here come the detours.

ೞ 8 ೞ
Detours

A temporary route used instead of the main route
Going off the main course into a roundabout way to get to the
same destination.

Coming across detours as we travel along is usually upsetting because detours force us to waste time going out of the way. Somehow we try to make up for that time by speeding up when we get back on the familiar route. However, when we speed up, we expose ourselves to the authorities an get punished for disobeying traffic laws. The same scenario occurs in life with our choices. We can make the wrong choice or take the wrong route and find ourselves on a detour.

One detour took me 10 years to find my desired route. Detours are nuisances and that's putting it mildly. When you're on a detour you say things like, "I started to …," "some thing told me …," and "if I ever get back …." Detours are completely avoidable just by listening and knowing when to take a chance and when not to.

When your life is going as expected and just as you planned with all your ducks in a row, suddenly up jumps the devil. And bring out the toilet paper because here comes the mess! You took a chance, walked too close to the edge, and now you're looking at a detour. You are suddenly pulled away from your ducks-in-a-row life into a nightmare detour and you don't know what to do but deal with it. Yes, of course, you have to deal with it, but you also have to stop moving on the right path to deal with the detour, a costly mistake that can take years to recover from.

Detours can have serious repercussions for innocent little mistakes or wrong choices. Okay, you want examples? I'll give you some examples. When I was 21 years old and fresh out of nursing school, I wanted to return the following semester to finish with the rest of the degree. I was creating my future, was still enthusiastic, and had a strong, hopeful vision. I also had an obsessive husband. After I graduated from LPN school at 8 months pregnant, to him school was finished, a done deal. He said it was time for me to go to work, be a wife, and mother—no more school.

He was binding and jealous so I rerouted my vision to fit his. I denied my dream and took his detour, which ended up in disaster because I was unhappy. Had I stayed on my path and not taken his detour, I would have been much happier. More than likely, he would have been happier too, because there would have been even more money for us to enjoy. He would have gotten over it and would have probably appreciated me more for taking a strong stance and having the strength to tell him no in order to continue with my personal growth.

That detour took 10 years out of my life. I was not a loser, however. I vowed to get something out of that detour if only to enjoy the view, and a delightful view it was. While on my detour, looking all sad and long faced, being the wife and mother I was born to be, opportunities came and left, but I was on a detour with no exit. I had another baby and thought to myself, "Now what shall I do? I'll never get back to school."

I tried to resolve myself to complacency, settling for my life the way it was, but the thought made me sick because I hated my life. I had an itch I couldn't scratch. My marriage settled and we moved to Puerto Rico. I was warned not to go because the move would be another detour that would take me even farther away from my goals. Friends and family told me "He is not a stable man" and "You should not go." I even had my husband's family members telling me not to go with him.

Yet, I saw an opportunity that no one else saw. Behind one of those cast iron doors of commitment, I went to Puerto Rico at 24 years old, a thousand miles across the water. I couldn't just drive back home.

Puerto Rico was beautiful in sight and dreadful in conditions. We were very poor and our living conditions were substandard. I thought, "I'll just get a job and we can live better." Well, when I found out I couldn't get a job because I wasn't bilingual, I was lost. I was on a real detour then, but I would not trade that experience. Living in Puerto Rico turned out to be very enlightening because it gave me appreciation for what I had and my abilities. After a grueling four years of recovery from five years on the detour from hell, I did recover. Here I am now.

Here's another example of a detour. A young man was left at home while his parents were going away on business. He was given specific instructions regarding what he could do and couldn't do. He was very positive and assured his parents he was going to obey. Well, after about a month of freedom, he decided to go out of town with his friends. He was a good kid, smart, one of the big men on the football team, headed for college, and an all-around nice guy. He had no record of trouble. He must have been feeling invincible that day because he was not supposed to go out of town, but he went anyway.

So, he and his friends went out of town (the detour begins) to the cliffs to jump. As they took their chances, one of the guys lost and lost big—he lost his life. The other boys panicked and were in fear because they knew they weren't supposed to be there. None of them knew what to do next, so they ran.

One of the young men lost his life and the others lost theirs too, yet they still live. They now have to live with the trauma and regret of losing their friend for the rest of their lives. Not only did the young man in question have to explain everything to his parents upon their return, he also found himself the subject of an investigation. After all that prepping and training, he still couldn't be trusted. He couldn't trust himself.

Later, he went off to college. Just when he thought he had put the tragedy behind him, he awoke from a dream that brought him back to the previous year's deep dark event at the cliffs. After an entire year had passed, he was still on the detour from that one little innocent trip to the cliffs.

Detours put your life on hold while you are on a temporary route away from your goals. Temporary because hopefully you'll return to your path no matter how long it takes. If you're 90 years old and can recover, do it. We learn on detours, a.k.a. the school of hard knocks. We can also learn by listening, obeying instructions, and staying on the right track in the first place, which is less painful and definitely more rewarding. When you stay on course, you experience your life more fully.

Are you on a detour? Are you doing anything that would put you at risk for losing your livelihood? We all have to get away from the edge before we lose our balance and fall into a detour. Detours usually do more damage the older we are because we have less time we can afford to waste. At 35 or 40, a 5- or 10-year detour could be devastating. At that age, we may not be able to recover emotionally from a detour lasting for such a length of time. However, if we really want to recover, we can show the world and ourselves that we can—that's good energy. However instead of using that energy and determination to recover, use it to reflect beyond your earth years. Visualize your future, in 5 years, 10 years, and so on, and make it come true. Do what it takes to make your way safe, bright, resourceful, loving, and peaceful.

When the fun crew comes around asking you to go do something daring, look within, remember your path, and in most cases say no! Doing something daring or edgy does not make you more of a man; it makes you more of an idiot. An idiot to put your life at risk, and also the lives of your parents and loved ones. A mature person knows how to conduct his life. He doesn't leave his life to chance. He is a goal-oriented and self-directed leader. Are you a follower or a leader?

I'm doing what I'm supposed to be doing as prescribed by my destiny and spirit. I feel confident about my future and it feels good. However, I have met individuals who almost took me on a detour. I had to recognize the flags and stay on my route. When I look at a person and study him or her, I ask myself if I can see this person in my future. Judging by the person's body language or aura, I visualize whether I'll be looking at this person five years down the road. You can determine how someone will more than likely treat you by looking at how this person treats other people (in your presence and when he doesn't know you're looking). As they say, "If a dog brings a bone, he carries away one too!"

It's very important for us to monitor our ways. We're losing our leaders, who are becoming as extinct as dinosaurs. We need another Martin Luther King, Jr., to represent humanity and extend a message of peace and prosperity for all. Could that person be you? Would you be surprised if you were the one? What if you employed the techniques in this book, changed your outlook on life, and then became a world-renowned leader for humanity?

Until we really start living, we cannot see our real future, our destiny. Not until you realize how long it took for you to get on the path to your destiny is the magnitude of the detour apparent. Do you know the story about Paul? Or more accurately, the story of Saul who later became Paul? Saul used to murder Christians until he became one, and a very knowledgeable one too. Saul got off his detour and on the right tract and became literally immortal. Now people all over the world know the story of Saul becoming Paul.

I hope this chapter has helped you to know yourself better and be more self-directed. Taking chances that are outside your life's plan is like taking a detour away from your life's path. It's important to know your spirit early in life so you know who you really are. We lose many would-be leaders to detours. Most criminals have tons of repressed energy that manifests itself in the form of a detour; they become murderers, thieves, or rapists instead of surgeons, administrators, and attorneys. These criminals then enter the prison system and get a college degree, write poetry, or draw beautiful artwork. These people are on a lifetime detour as a result of poor training, poor self-esteem, and a lack of leadership in their lives. Each one can tell you what he wanted to be when he grew up, but somehow he never got the chance.

Remember your vision for your life and remember your instructions for getting there. Don't allow yourself to be put in a position to jeopardize your future, your family, or your destiny. Don't live the detour life. Don't say, "I was going to be … I started to be … I wanted to be …." Live your life as you have described it to be in your vision. Say no to detours. Wake up and recognize the direction of your life. Are you going where you're supposed to or are you on a detour that will take you 10 years out of the way?

The world needs someone who's not on a detour to uplift our nation's spirit and propel us to higher levels, like Martin Luther King, Jr., and the other leaders who helped change the face of our nation to a more diversified one.

ঔ 9 ଓ
I'm Going To Live Forever!

Eternally, incessantly, ceaselessly, continuously...

I had an experience that catapulted me into the realm of everlasting. I was able to see my lifeless body as a statue, yet I was alive and still had a sense of reality. I could see, I could think, and I felt extremely well. A sense of freedom engulfed me. Real freedom—no time limits, no deadlines, no pain. I couldn't feel any of the pressures of daily responsibilities or any of our earthly nature. I felt like I was alive and living forever.

I believe we all have this freedom and we can have it here, now. I believe this is the message of eternal life for all of us. We can enjoy this life if we choose. Living benevolently creates peace and happiness. The more you give, the more you get. It may sound strange, but it's the truth. Try it! My out-of-body experience allowed me to exit my body shell, enter into my spirit life, and revealed to me that life is eternal.

It's amazing how the body responds to fear—the fight or flight syndrome. Your senses tell you when something is wrong or when you're in imminent danger. Some individuals have a feeling of doom just before they die. We can sense when something is wrong or different because the Spirit guides us and prepares us to respond. It's an automatic response from our parasympathetic nervous system. How does the parasympathetic nervous system work? Where did it get its information or signal to start operating? It receives its information from your spirit.

There is more than one way to live forever. We can become immortal by making our mark on society, leaving a legacy, writing a bestseller, discovering a vaccine, or introducing a new technology. Bill Gates is immortal, regardless of whatever else he does, because he gave the world Microsoft. Think about it. There are a number of individuals who will go down in our history books, good and bad, who will live forever because of the impact they made upon our society.

Why do I say that I'm living forever? Not because I've left some huge legacy to my family, but because I've been blessed to transcend to the other side and see myself alive. All I want to do now is teach others how to get to the other side, take a peek if possible, and return to share the truth of life.

Although I don't know much about reincarnation, I'm sure it can happen. Sometimes I feel like I'm Sojourner Truth, bringing individuals to freedom through this book. The freedom to know yourself and Who gave you life. The freedom to know how to enjoy your life and live it abundantly. Knowing your spirit is the best part of life. Once you start to develop your spirit and get to know yourself in the real sense, you start to listen as it guides, directs, and comforts you in the midst of uncertainty.

You've undoubtedly asked yourself what you should do at times and your mind begins to search for answers. If your spirit is developed, it will guide you to a sound decision. If your spirit isn't developed, then many alternatives will pop up into your head that may seem right. In this case, you should do whatever gives you the most peace. You should choose the option that gives you the most comfort, regardless of how it makes anyone else feel. Now if you have to make a decision based on or for someone else, then you must consult with him or her to find out how he or she feels inside about the possible outcomes and the peace he or she feels with your decision.

I dream of leaving a legacy for my sons. I would love for them to say, "My mom wrote that book. My mom started the new after-school program in our community. My mom taught at that school. My mom was a nurse at that hospital and she did some great things there." I would love to have that information follow me beyond my mortal existence.

Have you ever thought about what you could do to leave a legacy to your children, your family, and the world? I really do believe we can live forever if we want. Some live forever as mastermind criminals, mass murderers, and spies with all sorts of negative propaganda following them. No one should seek this type of legacy. It's discreditable and no credibility should be given to an individual who commits such a crime against society. Statements from these criminals should be privileged information for law enforcement only; they should not be paraded in the media. Sure, the public should be alerted about criminals for safety reasons, but not in a glorified way. There is so much going on in our society today that we don't have to turn murders and crimes into movies. I would rather see a comedy over a blood-and-guts flick any day.

Yes, I will live forever because I want to live forever in the hearts and minds of the world. I have made a commitment to myself and to my Creator that I will do whatever possible to make my mark on society while I am alive. I can't run track like Marion Jones (we know she's living forever like Wilma Rudolph), but whatever I can do I will, and I will continue doing until I am no longer breathing. This deep seed lives within me to continue my work.

When you find your spiritual purpose, you will begin to recognize your value in the world. Ask yourself why you are alive. People have died all around you, but you are still here. What touches your inner man the most? Are you living with compassion? If you are not living with compassion, you are probably more interested in what the world is going to do for you.

Well, my friends, the world has some pretty interesting things it can do for you. It can expose you to its elements. Mother Nature is unforgiving and you better know something about her if you plan to live in the midst of her elements with the expectation of getting something for nothing. The world does not offer up anything; you have to get out there and make it. We all have to give something of ourselves to get something, like time, our most valued commodity. In today's business climate, if you don't have a basic knowledge of reading, writing, and mathematical computation, you can subscribe to the poverty list. Some exit this bondage through dedication and application. We all have to get up, get busy, and prepare to live forever.

So, how does one prepare to live forever? Start with the first chapter, "The Application." Apply these principles to your life. Do the meditation portion to delve deep into your senses. Find out what makes you happy. Decide what you can do with your life vision to give something back to society so that it will remember you forever. Write a book, song, or poem; run for office; or push for changes on a community level. Mentor a young person or be a Big Sister or Brother. If you possess material wealth, give back to society. Make a monument on your behalf. Leave a legacy to your children or family. There are many opportunities for immortality in an earthly nature.

Perhaps one day when we all become acquainted with our spirits, we'll be able to communicate on a different level, by experiencing our spiritual beings with one another. Spiritual communication is so far ahead of our society right now.

Can you imagine yourself living forever now? Have ideas begun to flow into your being regarding how you can make your life count? Some athletes have made their mothers immortal simply by mentioning them as their role models who instilled the principles of morality within them, worked hard to provide for them, and motivated them to be the best they could be. Look at what Shaquille O'Neal's mother and stepfather produced together—a living legacy.

What can you do to live forever? You can pass on a life principle that will transcend time and trickle down through many generations. For example, a man could tell his son, "A man is only as good as his word." The son could then pass that living principle down to his son, and to his son's son, and to his son's son's son, and so on and so forth. This man's great-great-grandson will be able to proudly say that his great-great-grandfather always said, "A man is only as good as his word," and then stand by that with honor. This makes the family tradition strong and valid and the great-great-grandfather will live forever in the hearts and principles of future generations.

Yes, I want to live forever in any capacity that the Spirit allows me. I am driven to do something for the world. I am still trying and still moving forward in compassion and love. Despite hardships, I can still write, read, and speak. I will still be able to find a way to reach society.

We all need to know who we are in this world and why we have made it this far. We all need to know where we are destined to go. We will find out the answers by searching from within. What gives you peace and exoneration at the same time? What gives you the opportunity to excel inside? What drives you inside? What do you want to give back to society? How do you want to make your life count? By dropping this seed of immortality, I hope you will remember me long after I am gone. How can you make yourself significant in the life of another? Do you have that spirit in you?

There you have it. The best way to live forever is to give back to society—give some life to get more life. It's all in giving time, effort, self, and money if you have it. Yes, I did say money because some individuals do need it. You would be surprised at how you can change the life of an individual just by adding some money to his pocket; and he will remember you forever.

I believe giving of your time and yourself wins over money, though. There is something special about an individual being there sharing his spirit with another, which surpasses material gain. The effect of the giving of time and self lasts longer than money and is strengthened by matching a face with a blessing.

There are so many crooks out there nowadays; it's hard to tell who's scamming whom. This is where the Spirit comes in. It will guide you to someone you should help by placing the person in your path. Sometimes the person will object to your assistance at first. But by displaying a spirit of love in his or her presence, eventually he or she will soften up and move toward you. That's the power of love. It will find its way to the light, just like truth always finds its way to the light.

Here's an example. I had a friend who had a dog, Max, who was a mean dog (so said my friend). One day, I stopped by this friend's home for a visit, but he wasn't there. Max came charging at the gate, ready to eat me alive. I knew he couldn't get beyond the fence, so I knelt down by the gate and sat there with confidence and a real love for this dog, because he was protecting his master's lot. I liked dogs anyway, no matter how mean they were. Nevertheless, I just sat there listening to Max bark and growl, angering him by my audacity to just sit there and ignore his warning. Finally, he decided to stop barking when he realized I wasn't going anywhere, so he sat down on the other side of the gate next to me watching my every move. When I changed positions, he would begin to growl again.

After about 15 minutes of sitting, waiting, watching, growling, and barking at me, the dog decided to stop his fussing. After another 5 minutes, Max was looking at me and I was smiling at him. His tongue was hanging out and he was panting from being in the heat. I could see he probably needed some water. I got the squirt bottle of water from my car, took a long squirt into my mouth, then squirted a bit toward him. He started licking the fence where the water drops fell, so I squirted some water into his mouth. I moved closer to him and the fence. Before I knew it, Max was licking my hand and drinking my water. When it was all gone, he curled up by the fence next to me. I actually had the nerve to stick a couple of fingers through the fencing to rub his head, which he allowed me to do, and he licked my fingers as I pulled back. Soon my friend returned and was surprised to see me petting his Pit Bull Terrier at the fence. He asked what I did to get Max to let me pet him like that. I told him that I simply offered Max patience, love, and a drink of water.

If we offer obstinate individuals love, compassion, patience, and living water that they can survive on, they too will come around. I believe in the power of love. It is this power of love that allows us to live forever. It is the love that goes beyond the mortal living. It's what you feel when you are in the Spirit. Complete love is what I feel when I'm in my spiritual realm.

The power of love has allowed me to live forever and I thank the Spirit for choosing me. I am available for the work. Should my voice be the only one ringing out to the Spirit, so be it. Let it rise to the highest of highs. Let it move around the world, touching and telling the story of life everlasting. Yes, I am going to live forever!

ॐ 10 ಚಃ
Principles

A basic truth, law, or assumption
A rule or standard of personal conduct
A moral or ethical standard

The principles of life and love are governed by your conscience or spirit. Your spirit allows you to do what you do to your fellow man. I live by the principles of my spirit. They guide me.

The principles we live with on a daily basis establish our character. As mentioned earlier, I've always been told, "A man is only as good as his word." If you can trust a person's word, then you have come upon a person of integrity, longevity, and honor, who lives by principles.

Principles are governed by reconciling a situation with the truth. Principles are guidelines that you apply to your life to create a standard of living. We can make rigid principles liberal or live without any principles, like so many of us do. For example, upon arriving at work one morning, I secured a place at the desk where I usually sit by placing my belongings and my bag of supplies there. When I returned to my spot, a young lady was moving my things and placing them elsewhere. When I told her that I was sitting there, she said, "Oh! I'm sorry. I didn't mean to take your seat." All the while, she continued moving my stuff and remained seated there. I stood there for a moment, waiting for her to move away, but she never did. In fact, she made herself comfortable there, so I took a seat elsewhere.

I wondered, "Is she really remorseful for taking my seat or did she think her apology gave her the right to take my space?" The principle presented here is that an apology usually requires rectification. In other words, one must apologize and rectify what's been done. I should have gotten my seat back. She should have gotten up, replaced my belongings, and moved to another seat. Those actions would have led me to believe that she was truly apologetic about taking my seat. Instead, she showed me that she was selfish. I took another seat to avoid confrontation and contention, since we had to work side by side all day. My principles compelled me to not sweat the small stuff. I wanted to have a good day at work. I took the less favorable seat and indeed had a great day at work. She, on the other hand, ended up having a terrible day. "Fate is the Hunter," which will be explained in the next chapter.

Principles will always prevail when you examine a person's character. Examining a person's principles will tell you a lot about that person. Most often, the productive individual has the highest principles. Type A personalities usually have rigid principles because they seek perfection. If everyone had somewhat of a type A personality, we might have better public service. As you grow to know your spirit, you will develop a standard of principles and will find perfection along with frustration. You will discover that there are numerous individuals who do not use principles to guide their lives. Be patient with people who have few principles.

It is disheartening to find out that very few individuals care about public service. We depend on public service to get things done such as banking, shopping, and home management. Unfortunately, most policies within public service organizations are in place to prevent criminal activity. For example, today nurses must get fingerprinted to obtain a license. So when I had to put all this black gooey stuff on my fingers for finger-printing, I ask the assistant why they didn't use laser computerized finger-printing instead of the messy stuff. She replied, "Oh, we do, but it is too expensive to use down here for the general public." I replied, "Oh, so you use it upstairs for the criminals instead." She just gave me a strange look, realizing I was correct in my analysis. Honest individuals are experiencing restricted options because there are so many dishonest individuals who have not adopted any principles regarding what is legal, proper, and ethical.

In Chapter One, I talked about the fruits of the Spirit: love, patience, long-suffering, kindness, humbleness, and charity. These are all principles. If you're not applying principles in your life, maybe you should try. All you have to do is wake up and say, "I'm going to start operating with principles today, the first being truth, the second, honor."

It takes practice to use principles. Our selfish nature takes over and we seek our own benefit, basing our decisions on our own self-interest. We should use the blind principle of justice and do the right thing. There are people who are incarcerated for killing children or their parents. What's worse, there are murderers walking the street who are willing to do anything to anyone. Now that's scary! Those individuals need to have lessons in the principles of respect, honor, and truth. Those who choose to live without principles have lives that speak for themselves, just as those who do apply principles.

If I had to categorize principles, love would be number one, followed by truth, honor, and respect. If we all applied these principles to our lives, we would have a much better society. When society begins to accept all humans as one species of life, then we'll be able to enjoy life more. We would and should appreciate the differences we offer each other.

Apply principles that can bring peace and happiness to your life. Applying principles in all aspects of your life will decrease stress and free your spirit. You'd be surprised at how much easier decisions will be and how choices can be made soundly with ease.

To apply principles to your life, study yourself and write down what you will stand for. "I will stand by what is right regardless. I am going to keep my word from this day forward. If I am found to be in a position where I can not keep my word then, I will make restitution for it. I will not impose on the rights of others. I will respect each individual as I want to be respected. I will not ridicule my fellowman. I will hold my head up high knowing I have these principles to guide my character and how I treat those with whom I come into contact."

It will not hurt to add the principle of love to your daily regimen of character monitoring. That's right, we have to monitor our character until what we desire to be comes naturally. You will then be at peace and will be happy and free, but these things are not easy to obtain. You have to want them badly enough. You have to want to change your life. Principles are concrete and stand paramount in their own right.

.

ೞ 11 ೦෨
Fate Is The Hunter

*Do you think you can mistreat people, use people, and be self-
ish most of your life and prosper?
I tell you Fate Is The Hunter.
Do you think you can lie to people and not be lied to by people?
Fate Is The Hunter.
Do you think you can steal and not get stolen from?
Fate Is The Hunter.
Do you think you can cheat and not be cheated on?
Again I tell you Fate Is The Hunter.
Do you think you can hurt someone and not get hurt yourself?
Fate Is The Hunter.
Do you think if you never give to anyone
that someone is going to give to you?
Again, Fate Is The Hunter.
If you don't love yourself, do you think
someone else will love you?
Fate Is The Hunter.
If you have hatred, jealousy, envy, and contempt in your heart,
do you think you will survive?
You better think again because Fate Is The Hunter.*

—Terri D. McLennan

Fate is our hunter. It will hunt you down and hand you your destiny. Fate is actually what's left after all is done in a matter. If you stick your hand in the fire, you will get burned.

As we live our daily lives, we go along as if there are no consequences to how we treat people, as long as we're not committing a crime. We can be snotty, sarcastic, demeaning, or just straight-up rude. If the receiver of our negativity doesn't respond in an aggressive manner, we get away with our bad attitude.

We have very few morality laws; however, there is a higher law that few of us ever acknowledge. It is the law in the cycle of life. My e-mail signature reads, "Life is a cycle. Whatever you do comes back to you magnified." I believe our future well-being depends on how we feel today and how we treat each other today and from now on. Your fate depends on you. Your life does not belong to you, but your manner of living does. What you do to sustain your life and manner of living is your responsibility and will determine your fate, your destiny.

The Truth will find its own way to the Light, but sometimes it may take a while. Nevertheless, it will be vindicated in your life. The Truth, unfortunately, does not always win. When It doesn't, woe be unto the one who benefited from the lie. What we do in life will return to us. As we build doors for ourselves, we build our future. We can manage fate as it returns to us.

Why do bad things happen to good people? The answer is because there are bad people in the world. What made these good people deserve the wrong that has occurred to them? As mentioned in earlier chapters, when we don't listen to our spirit, we end up in the wrong place at the wrong time. Even then, we still have a door to go through to complete the transition of our lives. Reaching the other side of life is merely a transition. We all go there. I want to believe that when an individual is mutilated in an accident or distorted in death, his or her spirit left the body long before he or she would have ever felt the pain of the distortion.

I believe my son did not feel any pain in his death. His face was expressionless and he looked like he was asleep. He had no frowns on his face. His head was intact and his face undistorted, even though he died a tragic death. I'm not sure of what he did to deserve the way he died. He may have hurt someone. I do not know. We can never fully know the spirit and heart of a man.

Years ago when I worked in long-term care, I would wonder why some patients were bedridden, contracted, and unable to move. Some of us live our lives, work hard, grow old, and then have to depend on the person passing by to give us a drink of water. Some become insane and do not know who they are or who anyone else is. I wonder why this person's last days of living are like this. What kind of life did they have? Did they hurt someone along the way? If I treat everyone the way I want to be treated, will that guarantee me a peaceful life in my elderly days or will I even live to get old? Many people grow old cheerfully and mentally intact. Some grow old and become perpetually angry. Why is their life like that? It is their fate.

I cannot imagine myself becoming angry as I get older. I try to live my life as if I want all goodness to happen to me. I'm a visionary for my future. As I share my methods with you, I hope they will work for you too. I feel blessed and on top of my world. I know who the Author of my life is. I honor Him with my life as I guard my manner of living by listening, obeying, and having good things to say. I do it by uplifting my fellowman as opposed to being a busybody. I choose to think positively because I know Who holds the answers. When I see a wounded man or hurt person, I will help him if I'm in a position to do so. I will give that drink of water he needs. I am available to follow what the Spirit says and I'm doing my best to live at a higher level.

Living at a higher level requires work and dedication. I am working for my life, my fate. I have faith that the cycle of life will not return void. It will give me my due as I have given to others and myself. If I am compassionate, then compassion will be given to me. If I give, I will receive. If I love, then I will be loved. I will live by that faith. As a long-time nurse, my work has given me so much pleasure and an opportunity to be nice to people. I love being nice. Yes, it's a challenge to be nice to everyone all the time, but I have the opportunity to help in the preservation of a life. I get to say, "May I help you?"

Working in the field of nursing is different from giving up your life for a cause. Gandhi gave up his life for others. He stopped seeking his own way and started living for the wounded and deprived. He used a method that would work in his world and cause change. When his mission was over, so was he. Martin Luther King, Jr., gave his life to fight for the civil rights of African-Americans. Abraham Lincoln gave up his life for a people and a nation. Our fate will find us and give us a door to our transition to the other side. Once we are there, we will come to realize the vanity of our lives as we live through the limitations of our humanness

We live in a cruel world. People are naturally cruel. Children are cruel to each other. It's amazing how we can define goodness when so few exhibit it. We have laws for protection, to keep people under control and to maintain fairness, because we have cruel, selfish, greedy people in this world. Without laws, living would be even more difficult than it is. Fate is the hunter of us all. It's not a secret. Your fate is given to you as a measure of your manner of living

Fate is defined as a predetermined outcome or result. If we develop our spiritual lives, we can determine our destiny. We can know our fate. We may not necessarily know how we will die, but we will have no fear. Remembering the cycle of life will help you live your life for good. The human nature demands self-preservation. We cannot change the nature of our humanity, but we can apply control.

It doesn't hurt to be nice. If you don't know how to be nice to others, start with yourself. Be good to yourself, then apply the same goodness to others. If we love ourselves, being nice to others is easy. There are no guarantees in life, no matter how good we are or try to be; however, we can control some of the pain we experience if we seek a higher level of living by remembering our fate and avoiding things that will cause decline in our way of living.

Can we live disease free? Yes. Most of us are born disease free, so if we maintain a pure and healthy lifestyle and lead a good life, then, yes, we can have a healthy, long life. If you smoke, you're at risk for lung disease, so stop smoking. If you drive recklessly and too fast, you're at risk for an accident, so slow down. You know the drill. There are consequences to all of our lifestyle habits. If we apply life-sustaining habits, then we will sustain our life. Some say a life with no vices is boring, but when you're 60 years old, running a marathon or swimming five miles a day, your life suddenly won't appear boring. Everyone will want to know how you maintain such a healthy body.

At forty-one, I'm starting late, but nevertheless I have started a routine of healthy living. I will be faithful for another forty years of healthy living and will listen to my spirit as it guides me to my future, my destiny, my fate. From this day forward, I will build my fate on the rock of kindness, love, the edification of others, honesty, spirituality, and faith. I pray to get what is due me from this level of living. From this way of living, I hope to receive good health, peace of mind, laughter, love, and a legacy that outlives my mortal living. What more can an individuals ask for? What else is there in this life?

Oh yeah, there *is* the vanity of being rich. I want to be loved more than I want to be rich. I want to be remembered as someone who did a great thing in the life of another more than I want new clothes. I want everyone who reads this book to benefit from its message more than I want the material things life temporarily offers. When I'm old and gray, my new house is not going to love me. It will be seeking repairs or upgrades. When I'm old or sick, new clothes will not sustain my health.

Do you think our world will ever become a wholly spiritual one? If we each live a life of giving, caring, loving, and sharing, it can be. Exchange a life of vanity for loving and giving. You cannot beat giving. You cannot beat loving. The rewards from giving and loving are so great that they go way beyond your life and transcend time. Try it. I am and it's working for me. Like you, I'm just another person who makes choices. I am reaping the benefits of my choices and they are making me feel good. I hope you will feel what I feel.

We all need love, peace, happiness, health, and each other. It works for me, so it will work for you. Build a wonderful fate for yourself, a destiny prescribed by you and only you, with the help of God. Following the Spirit and remembering the cycle of life will help you discover your fate, your destiny, and the goodwill waiting for you.

ಸ಼ 12 ಚ಼
Living At A Higher Level

*Superior, reaching an elevated place or
situation above the baseline,
greater height than average,
or the mean above the standard.*

Everyday when I wake up, I want to feel my spirit. I want to know that I am alive spiritually and physically. One may ask, "How do you feel your spirit?" When I arise, I feel my spirit when I recognize that I am alive and examine my first thoughts. What is the primary subject on my mind when I arise to a new day? Usually it's something like, "Thank you, God, for allowing me to arise with a sane mind." Then I feel grateful for having one more day to practice being nice and of good character. With these thought processes in mind, I am able to live at a higher level.

When I get up and my feet hit the floor, I go to the bathroom, like most humans who are physiologically functioning properly. Then I look at myself in the mirror. I look at what I see and look at myself as if I'm looking at a foreign image. I'm not sure who thought of putting a mirror above the sink in the bathroom, but it was a perfect idea. It allows you to see your face first thing in the morning, before any influence has shaped it for the day. You can see what you look like before any interaction with anyone else and before any episode has a chance to put a smile or a frown on your face. Every time you wash your face and hands, you get to look at yourself.

While looking at your face, your eyes, your mouth, your complexion, and then again your eyes (the windows to your soul), allow your inner spirit to look at your physicality, as if it were someone else. By doing this, you can elevate your thought processes from the physical to spiritual realm. Developing the ability to separate the flesh from the Spirit will help you live at a higher level. When you begin to live at a higher level, you can focus on the reasons something occurred instead of how something occurred.

One morning I woke up, five days after having surgery, with the idea of living at a higher level on my mind. I could feel my spirit command my hand to write down the words on my mind. Initially, it felt strange, as if I was in another realm of life. I was in another realm.

Our spirit and our physical nature are so intertwined that we rarely stop to recognize the difference. What drives us to think and have experiences? We can begin to live at a higher level when we begin to recognize our spirit.

I love to wake up laughing. Laughing is the most wonderful feeling in the world. It provides spiritual energy and agility. Laughing will give you spiritual energy. If you can laugh all day, you will have spiritual energy all day.

When we recognize our spirit each day upon waking, we come to know a part of ourselves that demands acknowledgment. Living at a higher level requires us to live with truth. Knowing your spirit will help you to live with truth. Your spirit is the light of life within you.

Living at a higher level means living with compassion and love. Ask yourself, "Am I an example of my Creator? Am I an example of the love my Creator breathed within me? Or, do I make my life a lie everyday?" We don't live in a perfect world and no one is perfect, but we can practice being perfect. It begins with honesty. We can raise our standards for living. We can increase our expectations of ourselves and encourage others to do the same.

After spending three days in the hospital, I evaluated the care I received. As a healthcare consumer, I was very disappointed because there was a lack of compassion. The nurses were overworked, the hospital was understaffed, and perhaps a couple of the nurses were in the wrong profession. The nursing profession was started to provide compassion and caring for those unable to provide their own physical care. Years ago, women entered the nursing field because it is a noble profession, because they were caring, and because they saw it as a mission in being godly. These women extended themselves without prejudice. Their only gain was seeing an individual get well and knowing they had a part in the healing process.

In the 20th century and beyond, the nursing profession has attracted a group of individuals who care less about other people and more about making a living. Nursing jobs have always been plentiful, including the more than 20 years that I have been in the profession. Making money in the nursing profession has become more important for some than helping someone heal or giving care.

Providing good healthcare requires compassion. There are many in the nursing profession who are business oriented and have no bedside manner. They are not in the business for healing reasons, but instead for economic reasons. The profession is now flooded with these individuals because the need for nurses is so great; however, being a bedside nurse takes more than passing the state board exams.

When I was in the hospital, the care I received was minimal. I can count on one hand how many times my caregiver touched me with the exception of looking for a pulse. Some of the nurses never touched me at all. They did not converse with me other than trying to teach me what I already knew.

We must all remember that we need each other. We need the human touch and the feel of a compassionate spirit to help us heal. Without compassion, true care is compromised and so is healing. When we live at a higher level, we recognize our power and the effects we have on others. When we care compassionately, we can help others with lifestyle issues. We should never forget that we need each other. Even when we are living at a higher level, we still need each other.

When you live at a higher level, your discernment increases. You will be able to feel the aura of another person. There are times when you can tell when something is going on with a person that is close to you. It's profound when you can sense something wrong with a person you don't even know. When you can look into a stranger's eyes and can discern whether they are compassionate, happy, and loving or angry, prejudiced, and hateful, you are living at a higher level. Living at a higher level gives you the ability to discern others without judgment.

I love the blessing that has been extended to me—discernment coated with love and compassion. When I discern a man who is carrying hurt, pain, prejudice, and anger, my compassion increases. My first question is why is he carrying such pain. Then I wonder how I can help.

Have you ever thought about how many people you come into contact with daily? Not only the individuals you see in passing, but also the individuals with whom you actually interact or speak. How many of those individuals leave your presence with a good impression of you? How many of those individuals will remember you for life? How many of those individuals will want to have a greater acquaintance with you? How many of those individuals will you remember? We go through life passing people by like trees, never noticing how we affect them or how they affect us.

I really enjoyed the smile of the waitress who served me one evening. Her smile was genuine and her interaction made my dinner much better. I want to return to that diner again, not only for the food, but also for the service. How many times do we go out for food and if the service is poor, we won't return, no matter how good the food maybe? People do make a difference and recognizing this by living at a higher level makes us appreciate the next person even more.

How many lives have you touched today? Keep a journal of the people with whom you come into contact everyday. Indicate how each person felt when you departed. Were they smiling, crying, angry, disappointed, etc.? At the end of the day, determine whether you had a good day by the impact you had on the people with whom you interacted. How many did you make smile? How many were happy with you or had a fair impression of you? If you are able to keep the odds of those having a good impression of you at the end of the day at 10-2, then you could probably say you had a good day. If you didn't touch anyone in an entire day of being in the public or just outside your home environment, then something is wrong.

We all need people and you need people. Interacting with people is necessary for our well-being in this world. If we isolate ourselves from others, we will wither away in nature and personality. We need the interaction of others in the world. We do need each other.

Remember, we want to live at a higher level, so we must monitor our living. To determine if our days are profitable, we must pay attention to how we live each day. Our guidelines for good days or bad days must be determined by how we live and how we treat each other. Write down how many smiles you received today and how many arguments you had. Did you tell the whole truth? Did you hold back a message of edification because of pride? Are you jealous of someone else's success

Or, on the other hand, did you reveal the love of God within you? Did you tell someone how much you cared? Have you shared a word of prayer with someone in need of encouragement? Are you as positive as you could be in all circumstances? My definition of love for your fellowman is the unselfish will to do good for all people, in all things, under all circumstances.

Is it difficult to wake up everyday with the notion to love and project a positive attitude toward everyone who crosses your path? Are the writings in this book too difficult or too risky? Do you fear having this much humility? Do you believe you have to go around with a shield around your emotions to protect your heart and feelings from others?

We can live free of this bondage, free of trying to protect ourselves from others who really have no power over us anyway. It is your choice to live in fear or paranoia of others. We have the strength within to live free of fear and hurt. We know our emotions belong to us alone. If you are hurt, you must realize that you allowed yourself to be hurt.

My people, it is time to wake the sleeping soul. It is time for us to take control of our destiny and be who we want to be. It is time to stop giving our strength to others, only to suffer at their hands. It is time to live at a higher level. It is time to recognize who you are to the world, to yourself, and why God has allowed you to live this long.

About The Author

Terri D. McLennan was born in California in the late 1950's and moved to Texas in the mid '60s. She is the youngest child in her family. She faced multiple levels of adversity as a child and throughout her young adulthood.

After asking the Creator, "What is the meaning of my life?" she received her answer and spiritual enlightenment upon entering the spiritual realm through what is known as an *out-of-body* experience. It was through this experience and the death of her son that she gained the knowledge of living and the awareness of the Helper that guides all of us.

Terri is a registered nurse and has been in the medical profession for over 20 years. She is currently pursuing a graduate degree in advanced practice nursing. She is an officer in the Naval Reserves, has mentored young adults and adolescents, and continues to motivate and help individuals discover their purpose for living. She enjoys helping others, reading, writing, sports, and adventure.

www.ingramcontent.com/pod-product-compliance
Lightning Source LLC
Chambersburg PA
CBHW072025040426
42447CB00009B/1734